Machine Embroidered
Flowers, Woodlands and Landscapes

Machine Embroidered
Flowers, Woodlands and Landscapes

The Art of Alison Holt

SEARCH PRESS

First published in Great Britain 2011

Search Press Limited
Wellwood, North Farm Road,
Tunbridge Wells, Kent TN2 3DR

Based on the following books by Alison Holt,
published by Search Press:
Beginner's Guide to Machine Embroidered Landscapes
Beginner's Guide to Machine Embroidered Flowers
Machine Embroidered Woodlands

ISBN: 978-1-84448-345-7

Publisher's note
All the step-by-step photographs in this book feature
the author, Alison Holt, demonstrating machine
embroidery. No models have been used.

Printed in Malaysia

Contents

Introduction

Machine embroidery is an extremely versatile medium: it is easy to achieve wonderful effects of colour and texture with thread. In this book I will show you how to develop your skills and begin to create beautiful embroideries on your machine.

I first started experimenting with fabric, thread and the sewing machine in the late 1970s. My final year at college was spent working with vanishing muslin, creating collage landscapes full of winter trees. I coloured silk using a dye bath and cut it up to make my collages. Painting colours directly on to the silk instead of using pieces of material was a natural progression, and since then my way of working has evolved into a technique of 'painting' with threads.

I have been teaching textiles and embroidery for thirty years, and am as enthusiastic about machine embroidery as ever. The creative possibilities are endless, and in terms of scale and style of working, there is

Two Chairs
Actual size

The inspiration for this embroidery came from one of the gardens at the annual Hampton Court Palace Flower Show. The chairs were embroidered in zigzag stitch, a technique that stands out well against the texture of the gravel, which is worked in running stitch.

something for everyone. My loyal and enthusiastic students have always given me a great deal of encouragement, and I feel that at times I have gained as much from them as I hope they have from me.

At first, many people mistake my embroideries for paintings or even photographs. I am fascinated by gardens, landscapes and detail and enjoy the challenge of interpreting all the elements I see in nature. Inspiration is everywhere – in the effects of light on the landscape and in the juxtaposition of the amazing array of colours and textures in trees, foliage, flowers and plants.

Astilbe and Dogwood
Detail taken from original measuring 18 x 13cm (7 x 5in)

The complementary colours red and green work well in this richly textured study of flowers and foliage.

Daffodils at Chirk Castle
10 x 15cm (4 x 6in)

These drifts of daffodils are worked using a zigzig stitch, increasing in size towards the foreground to achieve perspective. This technique is shown on page 99.

I use two basic stitches: straight stitch and zigzag stitch, to make fine and broad brushstrokes on a hand-painted silk surface, blending both to achieve different effects. The raised embroidery on the coloured background produces a beautiful three-dimensional effect.

When I first started to paint directly on the silk background, I also began to take photographs instead of sketching. I like to observe detail and colour and analyse form at the embroidery stage, so I work directly on to the fabric using the photograph or photographs as reference – I am actually drawing with the needle. If you are at all worried about working straight on to the fabric, it can be helpful to make a sketch first and work from this, breaking it up into several stages.

The Mossy Wall
13 x 18cm (5 x 7in)

Spring foliage on the trees and autumn leaves on the ground supply the rich colour scheme of this embroidery.

Many beginners lack confidence in their ability to draw, but even this is less of a problem than you might think. Machine embroidery has a life of its own and some wonderful effects can be achieved without particular drawing skills. You could start by simply placing an image under the silk and tracing key elements of the design. As your confidence grows, you will find it much easier to cut out this stage and begin to draw straight on to your fabric before stitching.

I would love to take my sewing machine and sit embroidering in the middle of the garden or landscape in which I find my inspiration, but there are too many practical difficulties. This is why I find photography the ideal solution. I choose my location, then take a large number of photographs, combining or cropping them to form a base or starting point for my designs.

A word of warning: work cautiously, and experiment with different techniques as you go along, as machine embroidery can be very difficult and time-consuming to unpick. Keep some fabric stretched in a spare hoop, and use it to practise techniques before working them on your picture. Make sure the colour, length and direction of the stitches are all you need them to be for the effect you are trying to create. Finally – and most importantly of all – enjoy it!

Chelsea Garden
13 x 28cm (5 x 11in)

An award-winning garden at Chelsea was the inspiration for this embroidery. The composition is divided into horizontal sections, the central one being a painted area of closely clipped lawn which serves to break up the two areas of embroidery and to give a smooth background for the foreground detail. The diversity of plants in the border required a broad range of embroidery techniques.

Materials & equipment

Advice on the equipment needed for creative machine embroidery can be invaluable, for example the best sewing machine to use, the right size and type of hoop, which threads and so on. Information about materials, which may not be essential but make life easier or provide a shortcut, can also be a great help. This section aims to pass all this information on to you, to enable you to move on to the next stage of producing an embroidery.

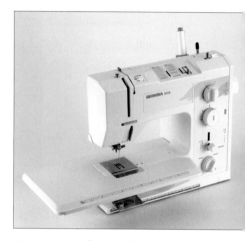

My sewing machine, with its table attachment and the presser foot removed.

Sewing machine

Creative embroidery can be done using any electric sewing machine. You can create more textures if your machine has a swing needle which does zigzag as well as straight stitch. A dial for controlling stitch width is better than push buttons as it allows you to alter the stitch width smoothly and therefore to 'draw' with a line of varying width.

Some sewing machines are set into a table, which is ideal. If this is not an option then a table attachment is important. It supports the hoop as you work, allowing you to slide the hoop around on the table. This is especially helpful when guiding the hoop with one hand as you alter the stitch width control with the other.

You can adapt your machine for embroidery by making only a few simple changes. First remove the presser foot. This will allow you to move the embroidery in any direction. Then lower the feed dog, which usually feeds the fabric through the machine in a straight line and is linked with the stitch length control. You will then be able to move your embroidery freely in different directions and at different speeds. This will enable you to create different lengths of stitch simply by varying how fast you move your embroidery; move it slowly to make small stitches and quickly for larger stitches.

Bobbin case

Some people are nervous about altering the tension screw on a bobbin case, and purchase a spare one to use for machine embroidery. The case should ideally be removable to allow easy access to the tension screw. Turn the tension screw clockwise to tighten the tension – this will keep the bobbin thread under the embroidery out of sight. Turning it anticlockwise will loosen the tension, enabling the thread in the bobbin to come to the surface of your embroidery and make it visible.

Machine maintenance

Some of the problems people encounter when starting machine embroidery are not due to inexperience but are caused by problems with the machine, which can be avoided if some basic steps are taken.

- A sewing machine needs to be well maintained – a machine that is serviced regularly will give you trouble-free sewing.
- Check your machine is sewing properly before you remove the foot and lower the feed dog.
- Always ensure the needle is sharp. A blunt or bent needle will create problems.
- Clean your machine regularly – lint will build up around the throat plate and needs to be removed.
- Check that the machine is threaded up correctly and that the bobbin is correctly inserted.
- Follow the manufacturer's guide for oiling your machine and do it regularly.

Threads

There is a wide variety of threads suitable for machine embroidery – as long as they are good quality and colourfast, which you use is down to personal preference. My favourite is a fine (no. 50), pure cotton thread; I like the fine weight and subtle sheen of the natural fibres. I always buy threads in tonal ranges as these are more useful for the way I like to blend colours in my work. To increase the range of colours available to me, I buy several different makes and weights of machine thread.

Silk

I have tried many different types and weights of fabric for painting and embroidery, and my favourite is a medium-weight, 8mm habutai silk. It paints beautifully, and you can stretch it really taut in the frame. It works well with the number and scale of the stitches my work entails, and it has an even weave and natural sheen which complement the cotton threads I use.

Other sewing equipment

Embroidery hoop

You will need a 20cm (8in) wooden embroidery hoop with the inner hoop bound with fabric tape. A bound hoop helps grip the silk more effectively, which keeps the fabric flat and taut during stitching and prevents puckering.

Machine bobbins

A selection of spare bobbins is useful, each wound with a different-coloured thread, because of the many colour changes needed during machine embroidery.

Screwdrivers

A small screwdriver is needed to alter the tension screw on the bobbin, and a larger one to tighten the screw on the hoop.

Machine needles

I always use a size 80 (12) needle. Make sure it is in good condition because a blunt needle will make pull lines in the silk.

Embroidery scissors

A sharp pair of embroidery scissors is essential for cutting threads close to the surface of your work.

Equipment for transferring the design

Source photographs

Photographs are essential; they are the inspiration for, and the starting point of, every embroidery.

L-shaped cards

These help you decide on the final size and composition of your design by allowing you to crop your photographs in different ways.

Air/water-soluble pen

This is used to draw out the basic design and details on the silk. It is air/water-soluble, which means it will fade gradually with time but can also be removed with water.

Resist

Resist is a clear gel that I use to mark the outlines of the basic elements of my design on the silk. It comes in a plastic pipette with a fine (0.3mm) nib, and when dry it stops the flow of the silk paints, preventing the background colours from spreading into each other. When the dyes have been fixed, the resist can be washed out with hot, soapy water leaving white lines in its place.

Masking tape

I use masking tape to attach my source photograph to the back of the silk so that I can trace the basic design on to the silk with the air/water-soluble pen. I also use it to hold the L-shaped cards in place when cropping the photographs.

Ruler

I always draw a frame around my designs to make sure the edges of the picture are straight and square, and for this I use a metal ruler. If you use the ruler to draw a line with resist, be careful not to smudge the wet line when moving the ruler away.

Silk painting equipment

Silk frame

I use a simple, square wooden frame to stretch the silk on for painting. This keeps the fabric flat and square, and raised above the table to allow the paint to spread evenly across the surface.

Silk pins

These are three-pronged metal pins used to secure the silk on to the frame.

Water pot

You will need a container of water in which to clean your brushes and to dilute the silk paints, making them paler in tone.

Silk paints

Silk paints are water based and can be used straight from the bottle to give the strongest tone, or watered down to make them paler. They can also be mixed together to make new colours. They are fixed to the silk by ironing with a hot iron once they are dry.

Palette

I prefer to use a white ceramic palette in which to mix my paints because it allows you to see clearly the colours you are mixing; it is easy to wash clean; and it does not discolour like plastic.

Paintbrushes

I use watercolour paintbrushes in a range of sizes from 000 up to 8. The larger brushes are for washes of colour and the smaller sizes for the fine details.

Paper towel

This is useful for removing excess paint from the brush when trying to achieve a fine line, and also for drying my brush after washing it to prevent the paints I have mixed being watered down.

One Bright Morning
18 x 18cm (7 x 7in)

The changing tones and colours within the sky are achieved by mixing all the colours you need ready in the palette and then painting quickly with a medium-size brush. This means the colours blend into each other for a smooth transition from light to dark. I used a different silk painting technique for the road. A very pale wash of paint has been applied first over the whole road and allowed to dry. Then, with a small brush and a darker brown paint, the shadows have been painted.

Working with silk paints

Understanding how paint behaves on silk is the key to successful silk painting, making best use of its strengths and working with its natural properties. My aim is to produce the same effect as a watercolour painting, though because of the way the paint behaves on the silk I have to adapt my technique. The basic principles are simple, and time spent practising will help you achieve the results you want.

Using silk paints

On silk, paint will naturally spread across the surface, so you need to control it if you want to paint in detail. Drawing outlines with resist will contain the paint within a shape, but to paint detail within an area and stop it spreading too far needs a different approach.

Starting with the lightest colours first, I let each colour dry before applying the next. This helps to give more control to the flow of the paint; as each layer of colour is allowed to dry, the paint applied on top will spread less and less. This allows fine details to be painted.

When painting fine detail it is essential to use small brushes. Experiment with different-sized brushes and see how far one brushstroke of paint will naturally travel across the fabric. Brush excess dye off your brush on the side of the palette for the finest painted line.

If we want areas of colour to blend with each other, both areas need to be damp. Wet the silk with a large brush and blot excess water with a paper towel. Colours should be mixed in the palette ready to be used so they can be applied quickly. I have found with experience that colours blend more successfully if you start with the palest tone and progress through to the darkest, overlapping each colour slightly.

For example, a field that shades to the palest tone towards the horizon should be painted from the horizon down to the stronger shades in the foreground, mixing all the colours needed in the palette before starting.

Fern Shadows
13 x 18cm (5 x 7in)

A pale wash was applied and allowed to dry, then the detail was painted on the boarded walkway with a small brush.

Mixing colours

A basic understanding of how to mix paint colours is important. In theory, all colours can be mixed from the three primary colours: yellow, blue and red. Any two primaries mixed together will give a secondary colour: mixed in equal amounts, blue and yellow make green, blue and red make purple and yellow and red make orange. If you vary the proportion of each primary colour, the end result will change. For example, more yellow than blue mixed together will make a lime/yellow-green, and more red than yellow will produce a red-orange.

When a primary colour is mixed with a secondary colour, the range of colours increases, and purple-browns, blue-greys and reddish-browns are created. These are called tertiary colours.

Hollyhocks and Pots
13 x 22cm (5 x 8¾in)

A rich mixture of stitched and painted detail was used to make this embroidery. It was based on a village in France full of flowers, narrow steps and beautiful, half-timbered houses. The decision to paint the stonework, steps and pots and to embroider all the flowers and foliage seemed a natural one.

Inspiration

Nature is a constant inspiration to me; whether I am out walking the dog or driving in the car, there is always something new to see: an unexpected snowfall, or an early morning sunrise with the most amazing sky contrasting with the dark silhouettes of winter trees.

The quality of light changes not only throughout the day but also with the changing seasons, producing an endless source of ideas for my work. I have my camera with me all the time, and I use photographs as a starting point for all my embroideries.

Using photographs

Photography is a great way of capturing and storing pictures that can be used as a basis for your embroideries, particularly if you cannot draw. I use photographs as a starting point for my own design ideas, as well as detail and colour references.

I try to compose my photographs carefully, interpreting the scene as a potential embroidery before taking the shot, but photographs can be cropped or joined together to improve the composition, or reduced in size to make them more manageable (I often make my embroideries the same size as the source photograph). Elements can be left out or moved within a picture, or parts of different photographs combined. Try taking the foreground of one photograph and putting it with the background of another; this can work very well. In woodland scenes, I often thin out the number of branches to open out a scene and make it less complicated.

New Shoots and Bells
11.5 x 13cm (4½ x 5in)

The source photograph, shown above right, has been cropped to form a portrait rather than a landscape picture. I intentionally made a gap between the foreground tree and those behind it. This opens up the picture, clarifies the position of the trees and creates perspective. More bluebells were added to the foreground using other photographs for reference.

Autumn Bank

13 x 28cm (5 x 11in)

The two source photographs, shown above, were joined together to produce the final composition. The hand-painted rocks combined with the stitched moss, foliage and tree trunks produce an interesting mixture of textures and techniques.

Cropping photographs

Effective cropping can add an extra dimension to your composition, helping to create the atmosphere you want the finished work to reflect. For example, framing your composition with a square or oval will help to create an intimate feel, while cropping it vertically can help to emphasise a vertical element of your design such as tall delphiniums.

Cropping also enables you to focus on just one element of a picture, eliminating unwanted sections and improving the composition. Experiment by moving two L-shaped pieces of card over your photograph, framing different sections until you achieve a pleasing effect.

The original photograph had the gate as a focal point and white flowers spreading across approximately one-third of the composition. I cropped the photograph to focus on the area of interest, and added poppies to the foreground to provide extra visual interest.

Cropping makes a dramatic difference to this composition. I was drawn to the spray of cow parsley in the centre of this scene, but its impact is diminished by the rest of the view. Cropping horizontally allows me to remove the unwanted elements of the photograph, especially the lower part, which lacks detail and interest, and focus more on the cow parsley.

Snow
7.5 x 7.5cm (3 x 3in)

The focal point of the source photograph was cropped out to form a small but strong composition.

A Sudden Fall of Snow
23 x 15cm (9 x 6in)

For this embroidery, the source photograph on the right was cropped at the top, then enlarged, and the distant trees were thinned out to reveal more of the sky. This created depth. The strong contrast of dark winter trees and quickly melting snow gives the picture a sense of drama.

Combining photographs

I often take many photographs of a scene: close-ups of different areas for detail and colour reference, and several overviews for composition ideas. This enables me to get a good 'feel' about the subject when I am deciding on my final design back in the studio. The embroidery of honeysuckle on the facing page is a good example.

To combine all the photographs for the final image, I first decided what size and shape I wanted the finished embroidery to be, which in this case was 13 x 28cm (5 x 11in). These proportions allow space for the two strong linear features: the tall post in the foreground and the silver birch trees in the distance. I placed the post in the composition so that it would occupy one-third of the vertical space. The other elements of the picture were fitted around it to create a balance.

A  B

First Frost
28 x 13cm (11 x 5in)

I loved the composition of photograph A, with the path leading the eye into the distance, the gentle curve of frosty grass cutting through the bracken and the stark winter trees, but I felt the right-hand side of the photograph was weak and needed a well-defined element to strengthen it. I 'borrowed' a tree from photograph B and made a strong, well-balanced composition with all the elements I wanted.

Honeysuckle
13 x 28cm (5 x 11in)

The photographs below show several views of the same scene, highlighting the different elements that I wanted to include in my finished composition.

The foliage of the silver birch trees was embroidered in a small straight stitch, moving the hoop slowly with a restricted spiralling motion to give stitches lying in all directions. Seven shades of green were used, starting with the darkest tone and working through to the highlight. The trunks were embroidered with pale grey on top and dark grey in the bobbin, using a closely worked zigzag stitch decreasing gradually in width towards the top.

The small pink flowers in the shadows at the base of the tree were achieved by putting pink in the bobbin and dark green on top, tightening the top tension to pull the bobbin thread to the surface and give flecks of pink within the dark area.

The fern and honeysuckle leaves were worked in a zigzag stitch of varying width, by moving the hoop slowly with one hand while altering the dial controlling the stitch width with the other. For fern, the width of the stitch was decreased gradually, while for the honeysuckle the width was increased to the centre of the leaf, then decreased to create the shape. The flowers are a combination of zigzag stitch and straight stitch.

A sense of scale

One way in which combining photographs can prove particularly effective is to help to give a sense of scale to your composition.

When you stand in a field of poppies, the sheer immensity of the landscape and the feeling of oneness with nature can be overwhelming. The problem of how to recreate that feeling can be overcome by using a panoramic view, combining two or more images if necessary.

In this embroidery of a poppy-filled cornfield, the long, narrow format complements the sweeping vastness of the expanse of corn and emphasises the absence of any human element. The pylon has been removed for aesthetic reasons.

Poppies and Corn

25.5 x 7.5cm (11 x 3in)

The two photographs on the left were overlapped to create one image. Poppies were added to create more foreground interest. The cornfield occupies two-thirds of the picture.

Garden View
127 x 305mm (5 x 12in)

For the composition on the right, which divides into roughly two-thirds lawn and one-third distant border, two photographs of my own garden were cropped and joined together. I took the foreground shot, then moved my camera carefully on the vertical to photograph the distance. Here there is a balance between the busy, textured flower border and the calm green lawn, which is predominantly painted.

Design

The first important step to producing a picture once you have chosen an image is to create a design based on it. Ideas can come from all around you – photographs, sketches and 'found' material. We are all attracted to different images, perhaps because of the colours or texture, detail or some abstract quality; we all have different tastes. It is a good idea initially to be guided by a tutor and to follow design rules, but to then go one step further and make something that is uniquely yours.

Composition

The composition of a picture is the way the various elements within it – shape, colour, texture and so on – are arranged. When composing your picture, try to create a sense of harmony, with all the different elements working together. Think about the shape of your design: for example, it could be a square, circle, rectangle or oval. To achieve a successful design, you should consider the following four principles.

Contrast

This can be achieved, for example, by combining different textures such as rough and smooth, shiny and matt, or hard and soft. For tonal contrasts use light and dark, or complementary colours such as red and green, purple and yellow, or orange and blue. Also consider the use of contrasting shapes within your design.

Rhythm

Rhythm gives a natural sense of order to a composition. It can be created by repetition, such as waves of bluebells in a wood or poppies in a meadow, or by repeating the same shape or colour along the length of a flower border.

Negative shapes

These are the shapes created between the various elements in the composition. They are a significant part of the design, and should therefore be given the same amount of consideration as the other design components.

Balance

The principle of the Golden Section relates to the idea of balance in an asymmetrical composition, and many of my designs acknowledge it.

It is based on our natural tendency to divide a rectangle or a line in the ratio of approximately one-third/two-thirds. This principle can be applied to a picture to determine where to place the focal point; what proportions of the various colours to use; or where to position the horizon. It creates a natural balance with which people will generally feel comfortable.

It is important to take into account balance and proportion when you are beginning to design, but remember that if you are happy with the way your design looks – even if it does not follow any recognised guidelines – you should go with your instincts rather than hard-and-fast rules.

Garden Door *(Above)*
18 x 13cm (7 x 5in)

The edge of the door creates contrast and a strong, vertical line, which divides the composition in the ratio one to two. Strong diagonals formed by the foliage lead the eye towards the back of the picture.

Foxgloves and Delphiniums *(Left)*
10 x 15cm (4 x 6in)

The shapes and colours of the flowers are repeated along the curve of the flower border, drawing the eye along its length. Contrast is created by embroidering the flower border and painting the lawn.

Colour

It is often the colours that attract me to a scene – I seek out bright, colourful autumn foliage with its complementary colours of reds and greens, and I love the strong contrast of white, blue, black and dark brown found on a frosty winter's day. These elements produce a sense of drama that will translate well into an embroidered picture.

Understanding colour

Having an understanding of colour, and how different colours are linked and composed, can help you identify the colours in your photograph and to translate them accurately into the threads and silk paints you need to complete your embroidery. For example, being able to distinguish a blue-green from a yellow-green will allow you to introduce subtle variations in colour, which in turn will result in a more realistic interpretation of nature.

Be aware that colours change, too, from distance to foreground. The muted greens, soft blues and grey-greens in the distance become brighter, stronger and more vibrant and with a wider tonal range in the foreground; this is where you find the lightest and darkest colours side by side.

Autumn Walk
16.5 x 25.5cm (6½ x 10in)

Rich autumn colours – reds, yellows and greens – give this scene huge visual impact.

Interpreting colour
in thread

Before I start to stitch, I gather together all the threads I need for the embroidery. To obtain the best match I can with the colours in the source photograph, I always do this in good, natural light. I start by choosing one colour within an area, such as a tree or a shrub, and then add lighter and darker shades of that colour until I have the full tonal range needed to replicate that particular element. I then move from area to area, repeating the process until I have selected all the colours needed for the whole picture. At the same time, I may make notes of what goes where, and this is particularly helpful if you are a beginner.

Reassess your choices at regular intervals during the embroidery stage, and be prepared to vary your selection – I often add an extra colour or two as my work progresses.

Achieving subtle variations in colour

If the perfect match in thread cannot be found, I mix or blend two colours together by putting one thread in the bobbin and one on the top of the machine, to achieve just the right shade. For example, if the nearest match I can find to a green within some foliage is not quite yellow enough, I put it on the top of the machine with a yellow thread in the bobbin, and pull the yellow to the surface by increasing the top tension. The eye mixes the two together and the green appears more yellow. Similarly, if a blue thread is the right colour but not pale enough, an off-white thread pulled up from the bobbin will blend with it and make it appear paler in tone.

This blending of colours by the eye is similar to pointillism in art, in which small, distinct spots of colour are used to create the impression of a much wider colour range. This effect will give your embroideries a depth and vibrancy that those using single, flat tones will lack.

To achieve blending and shading in my work, I change one colour at a time on the machine. A different-coloured bobbin thread can subtly affect the overall appearance of the top thread, as shown by the samples below. Each sample is worked in parallel lines of straight stitch, and I have used the same green thread on top for each of the samples. In the first sample on the left I have used the same colour in the bobbin as on the top, then, moving across to the right, changed it to dark green, pale yellow, white and mid yellow.

I find holding the reels of thread over the photograph works well, rather than just using a single thread.

    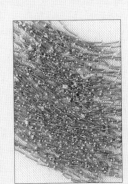

How to blend colours in embroidery

If the colour you want to use in your embroidery lies between two shades, the solution is to put one in the top of the machine and one in the bobbin. With small stitches and the bobbin colour showing on the surface, the two colours are mixed by the eye to the shade you want.

This technique (loose bobbin tension and tight top tension so that the bobbin colour is visible) is ideal for blending and shading, and has been used to create the subtle changes in colour and tone in the picture opposite. Notice that the more distant flowers are painted. They are 'suggestions' of the intricately embroidered foreground flowers, echoing their shapes and colours for continuity.

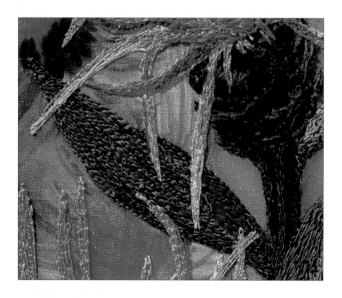

The petals above were worked in sections along their length, with the bobbin colour — mid pink — remaining the same and the top thread changing from deep to pale pink. If the bobbin colour is visible, it helps to blend the top colours together. The green leaf was stitched following the same technique — its colour changes from dark green at its base to light green at its tip.

The two petals on the left use the same shading and blending effects, but worked across the petal rather than along its length.

Knapweed (Centaurea nigra)
10 x 18cm (4 x 7in)

Parallel rows of straight stitch follow the curve of each slim petal. The order of work was important, completing the petals underneath before the ones on top. Observe the subtle differences in colour of each petal, and also how the colour changes within each petal.

The fruit pictures below have been worked using the same simple shading technique, which involves changing the top and bobbin threads independently of each other until the desired effect is achieved. Experiment until you can blend the shades of embroidery threads from dark to light or vice versa.

Victoria Plums
Actual size

Bramley Apples
Actual size

Raspberries
Actual size

Simple technique for shading

This technique can be seen at its best in the example of the Victoria plums above. To make it easier, lay out each colour group of threads from the darkest to the lightest tones before you start to embroider. The following hints assume that you are using four tones, but the technique works with any number.

1. Thread the darkest shade (tone 1) both on the top and in the bobbin and sew small parallel rows of straight stitch.
2. Change the top thread only to the next lighter shade (tone 2) and work the next section.
3. Change the bobbin thread to tone 2 and put the next lighter shade (tone 3) on top for the next area.
4. Put tone 3 in the bobbin and the lightest shade (tone 4) on top.

Changing and grading colours for shading works effectively when using straight stitch, with the top tension tightened slightly so the bobbin thread is visible. Embroidering a series of parallel lines works well for smooth objects, and a spiralling stitch gives more texture for foliage or gravel.

Distance & detail

In some of my embroideries I need to create an illusion or an impression, for example not every flower in a well-stocked border can be embroidered individually. A border of delphiniums, for example, would have a well-observed and executed flower or three in the foreground and lots of tall, textured shapes in blues and purples in the distance. This works equally well for poppies in a field or drifts of snowdrops in a woodland scene.

Foliage is as important and as individual as the flowers themselves. Look at and identify the incredible range of greens, from the deepest blue-greens in the shadows to the palest yellow-green highlight, and everything in between. A distant area of foliage is created by capturing the essence of it: does it have dissected or broad leaves, is its habit tall and spiky, dense or wispy? How widely do the colours vary? All of these characteristics need to be observed and will require a different technique.

In both the bluebells embroidery below and the snowdrops above, foreground detail shows each flower well constructed using closely worked zigzags. As the flowers recede into the distance, they become horizontal bands of colour, giving just the impression of flowers.

I am often asked what technique is used for a particular flower, a foxglove for example. There isn't one answer; so much depends on where it sits in the picture, and therefore how much detail you can see. A foreground foxglove, where you can see the individual trumpet-shaped flowers and many shades of pink, would require a totally different approach from a distant flower that is identified by its overall colour, shape and habit. The skill is in observation, for example foxgloves in the distance are tall, slender, tapering shapes that curve over at their tip.

Woodland Walk

Detail taken from original measuring 28 x 10cm (11 x 4in)

The middle distance foxgloves in the embroidery above are more simple in their construction than the foreground ones on the left. They are created with parallel columns of closely worked zigzag hanging down from the central stem of the flower. Working up one side of the foxglove stem and then the other, notice that the columns (trumpets) become shorter towards the top of the flower.

Foxgloves

This close-up study of foxgloves uses a combination of techniques. The trumpets are closely worked zigzags that gradually decrease in width towards the stem. These and the small buds are worked before the stem, which covers the connecting threads. With a darker shade in the bobbin and a tight top tension used so the bobbin thread is visible, the trumpets are shaded at the edges, adding to their three-dimensional quality. Where the zigzag is not wide enough, two overlapping rows are used.

33

Light & shade

This is a particularly important part of woodland scenes and, when used effectively, can create a wonderful sense of atmosphere and drama. The deep shadows cast by trees and their foliage, especially in winter and summer, give a strong pattern and rhythm to a design, as can the stripes falling across the woodland floor created by the sunlight streaming through the trees. Be aware of the direction of light falling on to tree trunks and foliage, be bold in your choice of colours, and use a tonal range that extends from very dark to very light. To create shadows in a bluebell wood or on snow, for example, you will need the darkest shades in your thread box; at the other end of the range, you will need white and off-white to create highlights on leaves or snow in sunlight.

Snowdrop Walk *(Left)*
13 x 18cm (5 x 7in)

Strong shadows falling across the snowdrops cause their colour to vary from white to blue.

Candy Woods *(Right)*
18 x 13cm (7 x 5in)

This is one of my favourite places at the height of summer, when the trees are heavy with lush, green foliage. I revisited this scene with my camera later in the year after a sudden fall of snow; the embroidery I created from it is shown on page 21.

Snow Vista

33 x 15cm (13 x 6in)

There is a wide variety of stitch techniques used for the different types of tree in this scene.

Creating backgrounds

I begin all my embroideries by transferring my design on to silk with an air/water-soluble pen, marking out the key elements and main areas of the composition with resist to control the flow of the paint. I then paint the background with silk paints. Simple washes are used to fill large areas with colour, then the details are painted on. Preparing the background in this way makes the embroidery stage easier and more logical, allowing you to focus on the sewing without having to worry about the sizes and the layout of the various elements. The coloured background also blends with the stitching more easily than bare white silk, which avoids the possibility of overworking the piece.

Here are two examples of source photographs and the painted backgrounds they inspired. When I have finished painting and the paint has dried, I use a hot iron to fix the image, then wash the silk in hot, soapy water to remove the resist. The white lines that remain can be seen clearly in these two paintings.

In the photograph on the left I identified three main bands of colour in the background which I separated with two lines of resist — the sky, overlaid with foliage; a bank; and the woodland floor. I then drew on the trunk and main branches of the tree.

The photograph above was also divided into horizontal bands, which I painted accordingly, and this time there are two trees, one more shaded and therefore painted darker than the other one. This leads the eye towards the bright patch between them, in the centre of the composition.

36

Transferring a design

There are several ways of transferring your design to the silk; which one you use depends on your confidence and skill level. If you have good drawing skills, the design can be drawn freehand directly on to the stretched silk, mapping out the key elements and main areas of the composition.

If you prefer, you can transfer the design by placing the source photograph behind the silk when it is stretched on the frame and then tracing over the top of it, again picking out the key elements and main areas. A light box is invaluable if you favour this way of working. This is the method described below. If not enough detail is visible through the silk, then use a tracing of the picture instead, made with tracing paper or acetate and a permanent marker, as this will show through the silk more clearly.

This demonstration is part of the project 'Fallen Leaves', which begins on page 112.

The source photograph for the design.

1. First, pin the silk on the silk frame. Make sure the fabric is straight, then place the first pin in the centre of one edge of the frame, securing it firmly. Continue placing pins along that edge, working from the central pin outwards. Space the pins approximately 8cm (3½in) apart. Work the opposite edge in the same way, ensuring all the time that the fabric is pulled firmly across the frame. Finally, pin the remaining two sides. If you can see strong pull lines between two sides, release the fabric from those edges and re-pin them with a slightly lighter touch.

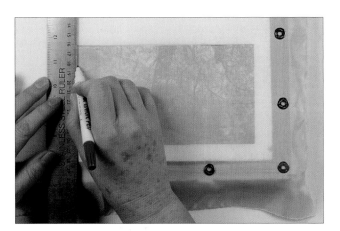

2. Place your chosen photograph under the silk, lifted up on a raised surface. It should touch the underside of the silk, so that the image shows through clearly on the top. Begin by drawing the border around the image using a metal ruler and an air/water-soluble pen.

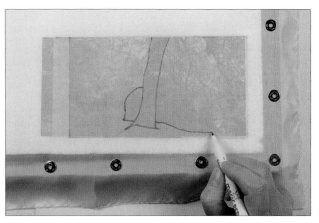

3. Place the main elements, in this case the tree trunk and the large shrub, by tracing around their outlines with the air/water-soluble pen.

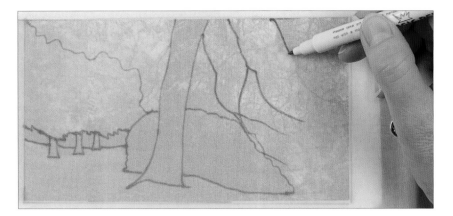

4. Next, draw in the three tree trunks on the left and the ground level behind them, outline the area of solid yellow foliage above, and mark in the positions of the main branches hanging down on the right. The area of yellow foliage on the left is larger than the section I have drawn. I will embroider leaves higher up where white silk will show through between my stitches for a lacy effect.

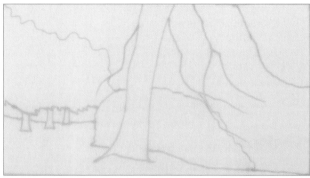

5. Remove the photograph from behind the silk and check that all the main elements are in place, and that you are happy with your composition. Leave out any details you do not wish to include.

Painting the design

1. Go over every purple line, including the border, with resist using a fine-nibbed applicator. Allow it to dry thoroughly. This will prevent the paint from spreading into adjacent areas.

2. Decide which area you wish to paint first, in this case the woodland floor. Using the photograph for reference, mix a suitable colour in the palette and test it on the silk before applying it to your background (remember that it will dry paler).

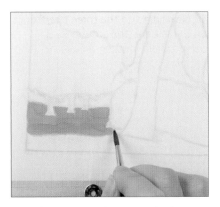

3. When you are happy with the colour (it does not have to be an exact match as you will be stitching over it), apply it as a flat wash to the background. Allow the paint to spread naturally up to the line of resist to fill the area you are painting completely.

4. Paint in the remaining large areas of colour – I have used an undiluted dark brown mix for the main trunk and the area behind the trees in the background, a dilute yellow-brown for the golden foliage on the left, and a strong green for the lower part of the shrub.

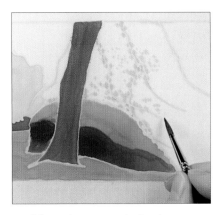

5. Dilute the green mix for the top part of the shrub, and use the same colour to 'dot in' the green leaves behind the main branches on the right. Place them either side of the branches to help retain a guide line, and to give depth to the finished embroidery.

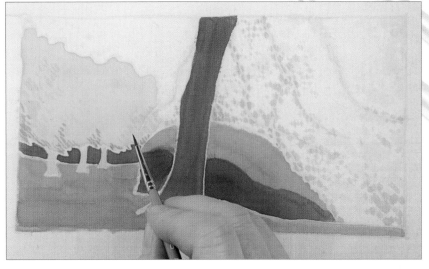

6. Dot in the yellow leaves on the right-hand side of the picture in the same way, and finish by adding dots of yellow and green to the golden foliage on the left, giving it a more three-dimensional feel.

To fix the image

The background now needs to be fixed with a hot iron and washed in hot, soapy water to remove the resist. Dry and iron the silk once more, and it is then ready to be embroidered.

Freehand painting

A background wash in silk paint serves well as the base for an embroidered winter tree. The source photograph was taken in January as the sun was coming up and the colours were changing by the minute. Experiment with sunrises and sunsets in pinks, purples and reds for a dramatic backdrop to a dark grey copse of trees.

By applying the silk paint to the silk without drawing out the design using resist, the colours can flow and blend into each other freely, creating soft edges to each area of colour. It is best to have all the colours you intend to use mixed ready in the palette before you start, so that you can work quickly.

A silhouette of bare branches set against a colourful, early morning sky. This will be worked as a network of lace in dark grey thread across a hole cut in fabric stretched in a hoop.

1. Begin by drawing the border for the picture on silk, pinned on to a silk frame, using an air/water-soluble pen. Then make all the colour mixes you think you will need, using the photograph for guidance. Test the colours by placing dots of paint on the silk and allowing it to dry.

Tip

Add more water to a mix for a paler colour; use undiluted paint, straight from the bottle, for a more intense colour.

Tip

When freehand painting, always work with the source photograph alongside and refer to it constantly.

2. Begin the painting by laying down the bands of background colour, starting with the palest. In this case, begin with the band of pale orange across the lower part of the picture, then introduce a little yellow on the right. Use smooth, horizontal brushstrokes, and allow the paint to spread and blend naturally on the silk.

Tip

Always clean and dry your brush in clean water when changing from one colour to another. This prevents unwanted colour mixing and prevents the colours from becoming diluted.

Tip

Work quickly, so that the colours blend freely on the silk while still wet.

3. Without allowing the first colour to dry, introduce the next band of colour (pale blue), blending it carefully with the first using the paintbrush.

4. Next put in the top band of colour – the darker blue across the top of the sky – and blend it with a narrower band of pale orange placed above the light blue.

5. Continuing quickly, introduce more of the pale orange into the blue. Blend some stronger orange into the lighter areas.

6. Bring in the purple tones to deepen the clouds in the top part of the sky. Deepen the lower part of the sky by adding more streaks of orange and yellow.

7. Allow the background to dry and start to strengthen the colours, beginning with the deep purple and orange tones in the main cloud. Use small dots of colour so that they blend in easily.

8. Once dry, continue to strengthen the purple until you have achieved the required depth of colour. Heighten the intensity of the lower part of the picture by introducing patches of pale purple and orange using a tiny brush. Fix the paint with a hot iron.

Creating the silhouette

Stretch some muslin or lightweight calico in a 20cm (8in) hoop. Cut a circular hole 10cm (4in) across in the centre and then re-stretch the fabric; the hole will increase in size as the fabric becomes taut in the hoop. With the machine set on straight stitch, pull up the bobbin thread through the fabric and start stitching across the hole. Move the hoop at a steady pace and simply let the top and bobbin threads twist together across the hole.

Tip

Do not zigzag to the top of the tree – the stitching will look too heavy.

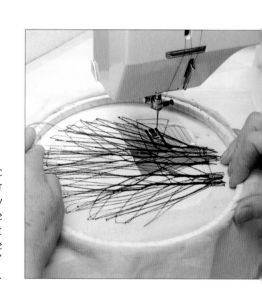

1. Start with a fan-shaped arrangement of straight stitches as the basic structure for the trees, then use zigzag stitch to gather the threads together at the base to form five trunks. Create more branches higher up the trees by criss-crossing the embroidery with straight stitching. Gather some of these together with zigzag stitch. Extend single lines of straight stitching just beyond the top of the tree for a more natural look. Once you have a shape you are happy with, work over it slowly with zigzag stitch to neatly 'bind' the threads together.

2. Cut the lace tree away from the fabric.

3. Stretch the painted background in the bound hoop and pin the tree in place, using the photograph for reference. Stitch it in place using the same thread as you used for the tree.

4. Using straight stitch, work V shapes up and down the top 2cm (¾in) of the branches to hold the silhouette in position. At the same time, create more depth by stitching new, smaller branches on to the background in between the existing ones.

5. Stitch across the base of the trees to secure them.

6. Work series of straight stitches using jagged and spiralling movements of the hoop to create the foliage at the base of the trees.

The completed embroidery.

43

Starting to stitch

A few small adjustments to your sewing machine will be needed before you can use it for creative embroidery.

Removing the presser foot

Removing the presser foot gives you an unobstructed view of your embroidery. Its normal function is to keep the fabric flat on the bed of the machine, but in machine embroidery the fabric is held flat by the hoop in which it is stretched. Remove the presser foot by unclipping or unscrewing it from the base of the presser bar. Some manufacturers recommend using a darning or embroidery foot on the machine, but this is not really necessary.

Lowering the feed dog

This allows you to move your embroidery in any direction and at any speed. Usually there is a dial or switch for lowering the feed dog, which on some machines is the same setting as for darning. If you cannot lower the feed dog, your machine may have a raised plate that fits over the moving teeth. If neither of these is possible, set the stitch length to zero. Each of these options will achieve the same result.

Tension of the threads

In conventional machine stitching, the tension of the top thread needs to be balanced with that of the bobbin thread to form the perfect stitch. With machine embroidery, you can create a range of textures and effects by simply altering the tensions. To change the tension of the bobbin thread, and therefore the flow of thread from the bobbin, there is a tension screw on the bobbin case. To obtain a neat, flat stitch with the top thread but not the bobbin thread showing, turn the tension screw clockwise. This will tighten the tension and restrict the flow of the thread, so it won't show on the surface of the fabric. This is ideal for creating fine detail with the least amount of texture.

The amount of bobbin thread showing on the surface can be increased by tightening the tension of the top thread. Turn the dial or lever to a higher number or towards the plus sign. For a more exaggerated effect, loosen the bobbin tension too (turn the screw anticlockwise). This can be used to create a highly versatile, textured effect, which can be varied by changing the way you move the hoop and by setting your machine on either straight or zigzag stitch.

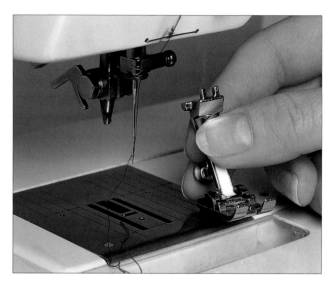

Removing the presser foot. Notice that the feed dog has been lowered so that it is no longer visible.

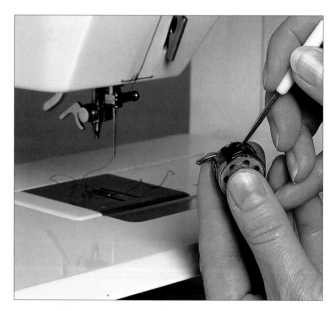

Turning the tension screw on the bobbin.

Binding the hoop

Before you start to embroider, bind the inner hoop with cotton tape. This will help it grip the fabric more effectively.

Stretching the fabric in the hoop

When stretching your fabric in the hoop, it is important to have the fabric really taut as this prevents the stitches from puckering the fabric and allows the machine to stitch properly. Usually, if the machine appears to miss stitches, which will result in the thread breaking, it is due to the fabric not being stretched tightly enough.

Starting to embroider

Place your hoop under the machine. Remember that you will be working with the hoop 'upside down' so that the back of the fabric lies flat on the bed of the machine and the correct side of the embroidery is face up. Lower the presser bar to engage the top tension so that you don't create loops of thread on the back of your work.

For the best control of the hoop, rest your forearm or wrist on the table so that all the movement required to control the hoop is in the fingers. Think of the hoop as a pencil with which you are drawing. Keep your fingers on the hoop, safely out of the way of the needle, and move the hoop around under the needle. This will become more controlled with practice.

Binding the inner hoop.

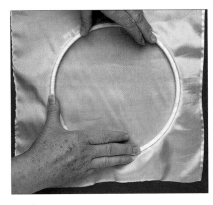

Stretching the fabric in the hoop.

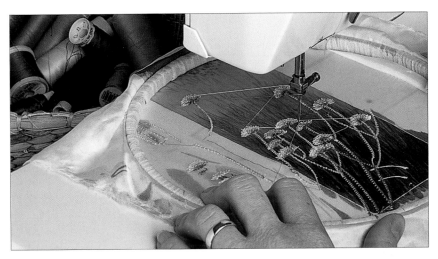

The correct way to hold the hoop under the machine.

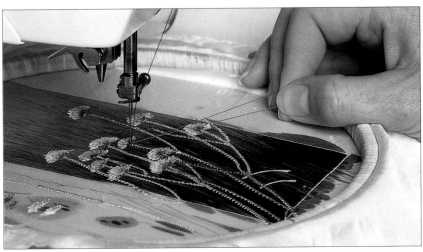

Always pull up the bobbin thread through the embroidery and hold it with the top thread to prevent them tangling. You can cut off these threads after you have worked a few stitches.

Stitch techniques

My embroideries are all worked in a combination of straight and zigzag stitches. Variations of each are achieved by changing the direction and speed at which the hoop is moved, and by altering the tension of the top and bobbin threads.

The length of straight stitch is influenced by the speed at which the hoop is moved: move it slowly to produce small stitches and quickly for longer stitches. Different hand movements also influence the result. Experiment by moving the hoop in parallel lines, in small circles or from side to side.

The appearance of zigzags is also changed by the speed and direction in which the hoop is moved. An advantage of zigzag stitch is that you have a choice of widths of 'line' to draw or experiment with. If you hold the hoop still you can build up, stitch by stitch, a machine embroidered 'French knot'.

When you add in the facility to change tension to these methods of varying the stitch, the range of marks and textures you can create is endless.

Analyse each element of your picture and decide the colour, direction and size of each stitch needed to create the effect you want. Experiment with straight or zigzag stitches, using a variety of hand movements and tensions, to see what you can achieve. Small stitches in the distance create a sense of scale, while larger stitches used in the foreground will give perspective to your work.

Azaleas
Actual size

I was fascinated by the shapes of the trunks and branches of these azaleas. They are embroidered in closely worked zigzag stitch which narrows in width towards the top. The leaves are also zigzag, and are created by increasing the width of the stitch to the middle of the leaf, then decreasing it to the end. The fallen petals are zigzags worked on the spot, with straight stitch between them to cover the connecting thread.

Basic stitches

My approach to machine embroidery is to think like a painter, and use the sewing machine as a paintbrush. This is how I turn my source photograph into an embroidery: I think in stitch. The sewing machine can only give me a fine line with straight stitch or a broad line when set on zigzag, and I use these stitches in a variety of sizes, directions and colours to achieve different effects.

Straight stitch

Use straight stitch to draw fine lines using either small or large stitches; and for fine texture, it makes a wonderful filler stitch. Experiment with various speeds and types of movement of the hoop to obtain different effects.

This sample has a red thread on the top of the machine and a yellow bobbin thread pulled to the surface by a tight top tension.

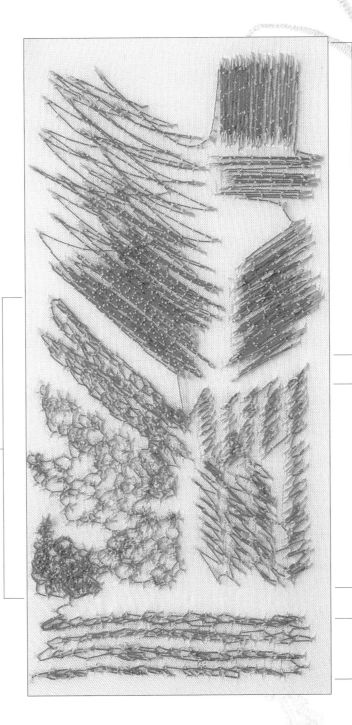

Parallel rows of straight stitch worked horizontally, vertically or diagonally, in straight lines and in curves.

Spiralling hand movements create a fine overall texture. The spirals can be round or lozenge-shaped, and worked in curves, horizontally or diagonally to fill in any shape.

A small, jagged hand movement gives small, jagged stitches that can be worked in any shape or direction.

Horizontal, spiralling hand movements.

Zigzag stitch

This gives a bolder, broader line to draw with than straight stitch, and is very versatile. It can be smooth or textured, worked in broken marks or in a continuous line, and placed lying in different directions by rotating the angle of the hoop. Remember to experiment with altered tensions and various widths of zigzag.

A narrow width of zigzag and the hoop moved slowly along a curved line.

Use a wider zigzag and work the stitches on the spot by holding the hoop still for the stitches to build up on top of each other. Move the hoop a short distance and repeat.

The widest zigzag stitch is used here. Place the stitches in various directions and overlapping each other.

Moving the hoop at a constant speed in a diagonal curve.

Moving the hoop at a slow and consistent speed in a vertical direction gives a column of zigzag; these can be various widths, straight or curved.

Zigzag stitch, varying width

To change the stitch width as you sew, use one hand to move your embroidery under the needle, and the other to gradually turn the dial on the machine (this technique is harder to master on a machine with push-button controls). If spaces appear between the stitches, move the hoop more slowly; if the stitching becomes too textured, move it faster. Using a darker bobbin thread and bringing it to the surface by tightening the top tension creates a more three-dimensional effect.

Move the hoop at an angle to make the zigzag stitches tilt within the shape.

Vary the speed of the hoop to alter the spacing of the stitches, and vary the stitch width to form shapes. Rotate the hoop 90° to lay the stitches horizontally.

Work columns that decrease in width as you approach the top. You can form several branches using this method.

Zigzags of varying width worked in curved shapes, both horizontally and vertically, and overlapping each other.

Flowers & foliage

This chapter is a guide to drawing flowers and their foliage with a sewing machine, using colour, line and texture on a delicate scale. It has wonderful possibilities and potential for the beginner as well as for the more experienced embroiderer.

I am a keen gardener; it's a wonderful contrast to sitting indoors at a sewing machine for many hours at a time. A lot of the photographs and embroideries in this book are based on the three-dimensional creation outside my house: my garden. It is a constant source of inspiration for me. I grow foxgloves, delphiniums, rhododendrons, irises, alliums, roses and much more, and try to create groupings of plants and views with embroideries in mind. As I weed or deadhead, I look at all the different flowers and imagine the techniques I could use on the machine to recreate them in stitch. My visits to the Chelsea and Hampton Court flower shows as an exhibitor give me wonderful opportunities to collect ideas for my garden as well as my embroideries.

My aim is to create embroidered flowers, each one unique. It is achieved by analysing the shapes and colours of the flowers and breaking down the embroidery into simple steps. I decide whether straight stitch or zigzag will provide the technique I need, or perhaps a combination of the two. I also consider the direction, length and colour of stitch that I will use. With the help of this chapter, I hope that you too will find the inspiration and technical know-how you need to create your own embroidered flowers.

Creating flowers and foliage in stitch

You can group flowers into types based on their shape or construction, and once a hand movement or technique is mastered for one flower in that group it can be modified slightly and the colours changed to create another. For example, similar techniques can be used for peonies, roses, hydrangeas and rhododendrons. With a change of colour and overall shape, the technique for a laburnum flower is repeated for a delphinium. The list below groups flowers and foliage according to common techniques. These have been divided into two categories, straight stitch and zigzag.

Straight stitch techniques

For plumes of grasses and foliage for flowers, use a jagged straight stitch worked in a column up one side, then down the other in a straight line or a curve.

Alliums, agapanthus, globe thistles and echinops all share characteristics — use a spiky straight stitch radiating out from a central point.

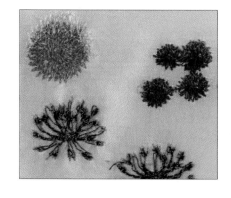

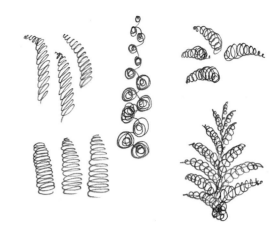

Distant delphiniums, lupins, foxgloves, hollyhocks, buddleia, ligularia, lilac (syringa) and foreground astilbe are created using spiralling columns of straight stitch.

Large, multi-petalled flowers such as roses, peonies and clematis in the distance, created with a small, spiralling straight stitch, starting in the centre and making larger stitches towards the outside of the flower.

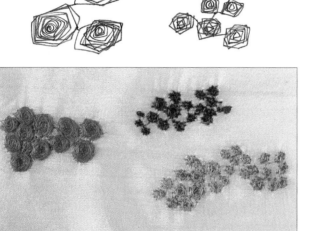

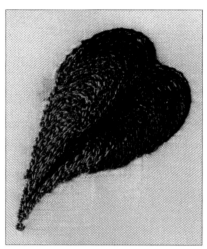

Large-petalled flowers such as iris, poppy and hibiscus, in the foreground, should be treated in the same way as broad-shaped leaves. Use parallel rows of straight stitch following the shape of the petals. Subtle colour changes and shading can be handled with this technique.

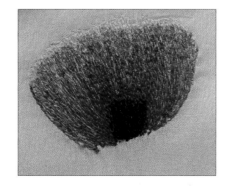

Broad, lance-shaped leaves such as laurel, rhododendron, hosta and foxglove, in the foreground, produced using parallel rows of straight stitch following the contours of the leaves. This will allow shading with a tonal range of threads.

Long strap-like leaf shapes, found with irises, phormium and gladioli, produced by parallel rows of straight stitch, closely worked.

For middle-distance crocosmia and irises, use straight stitch drawing along the shape of the flower.

Zigzag stitch techniques

Distant snowdrops, crocuses and daffodils created with vertically placed zigzags worked on the spot. Turn the picture 90° to place the zigzag vertically.

Middle-distance daffodils and foreground snowdrops and crocuses created with V-shaped sets of zigzags.

Mound-forming plants with small-headed flowers such as lobelia, santolina, potentilla and aubrietia are created with small zigzags worked on the spot in a curved shape. Slowly rotate the hoop a little to place the zigzags at the right angle.

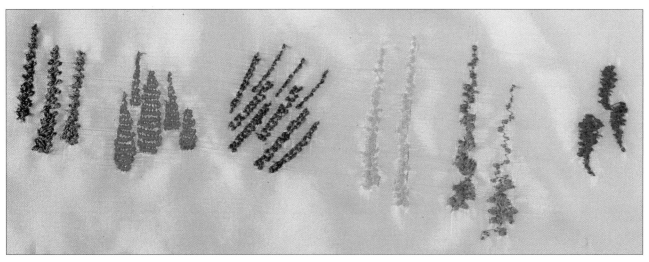

Tall, narrow flowers are created using small zigzags worked on the spot and grouped together in various ways to create different shapes.

Lupins

Delphiniums

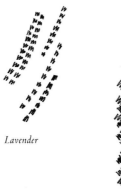
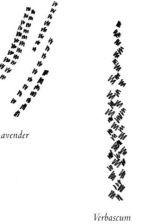

Lavender

Verbascum

Hollyhocks

Wisteria or laburnum

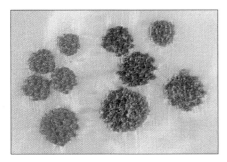

Round-headed flowers, such as phlox, hydrangea, azalea, peony, euphorbia and rhododendron, are worked in clusters of small zigzags on the spot, all facing different directions. This is achieved by altering the angle of the hoop.

Achillea

Flat-headed flowers such as achillea, cow parsley and sedum — use small zigzags worked in horizontal clusters.

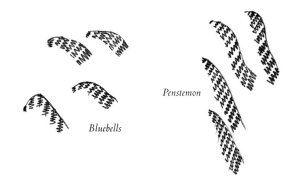

Penstemon

Bluebells

Tubular, bell-shaped flowers such as penstemon, distant foxgloves, bluebells, crocosmia, campanula and nicotiana are created using narrow columns of closely worked zigzags in diagonal parallel lines.

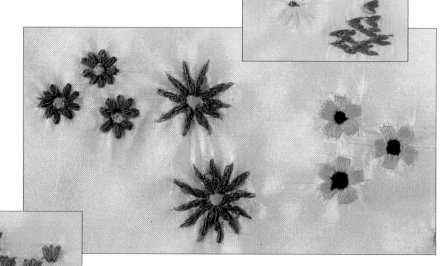

For star-like flowers, for example wild garlic, asters, anemone, oxeye daisy, Magnolia stellata and jasmine, use zigzag stitch rotated around a central point. With the needle in the centre of the flower, rotate the hoop a few degrees and work zigzag on the spot. Repeat until the flower is completed. Finally add a small zigzag in the centre.

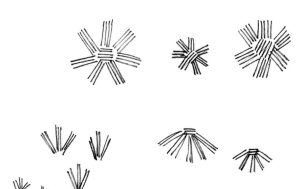

Foxgloves

This is created by altering the width of zigzag along the length of each trumpet. Straight stitch up the central stem and down a trumpet, zigzag back to the stem and repeat, increasing the size of the trumpets towards the base of the flower.

56

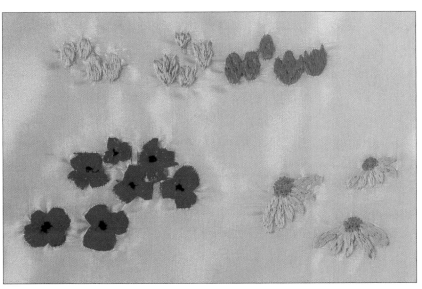
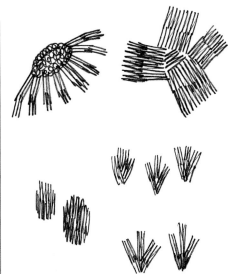

For larger flower heads in the foreground of a picture, use a double row of zigzag, for example tulips, crocuses, poppies and daisies. A spiralling straight stitch works well for the centres.

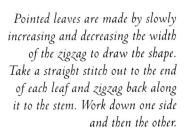

Pointed leaves are made by slowly increasing and decreasing the width of the zigzag to draw the shape. Take a straight stitch out to the end of each leaf and zigzag back along it to the stem. Work down one side and then the other.

For long, strap-like leaf shapes in the foreground, use closely worked zigzag with the width decreasing along its length. Leaves can be made as large as necessary with this method by laying several lines of zigzag side-by-side.

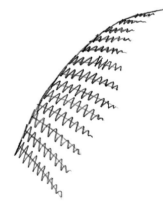

Ferns in the foreground are created with openly worked zigzag with the width changing along the length of the fronds. Start with the stem and work straight stitch out from it, then zigzag back to the stem increasing the width of the zigzag as you go.

For broad, lance-shaped leaves such as laurel, rhododendron, hosta and foxglove, in the middle distance or foreground, use closely worked zigzag with the width increasing and decreasing along its length. A double row of zigzag will give more width to the leaves and echo their natural form. Angle the hoop so the zigzag sits diagonally within the leaf shape.

For broad, lance-shaped leaves such as laurel and rhododendron in the middle distance, use zigzag worked on the spot in various sizes, lying in different directions.

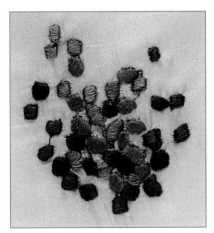

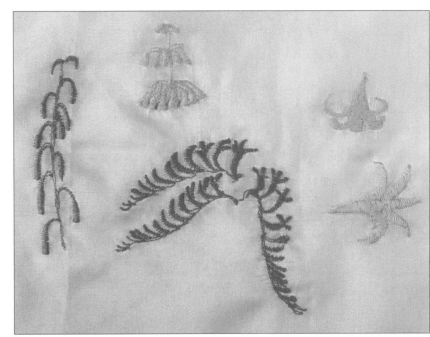

Trumpet-shaped flowers, such as day lilies, crocosmia and Candelabra primula, are created using closely worked zigzag, decreasing in width towards the flower stem, moving the hoop in a curved line. Work straight stitch out from the stem, and zigzag back.

Rounded leaves are created by quickly increasing and decreasing the width of the zigzag to draw the shape.

59

Combining techniques

Foreground French lavender, created using two techniques combined — a V-shaped pair of zigzag stitches and a short column of spiralling straight stitch.

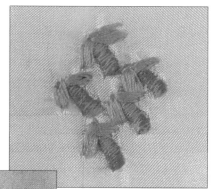

Foreground daffodils formed with a column of zigzag for the trumpet and V-shaped zigzags for the petals. The deeper shade of yellow is pulled up from the bobbin with a tight top tension.

Leaves with serrated edges, for example holly. First, zigzags are worked on the spot with the needle placed on the outer edge of the leaf. Next, a column of zigzag is worked down one half of the leaf, increasing in width at the centre. Finally, this is repeated down the other side of the leaf.

A combination of curved straight stitch was used to form the basic shape of the allium or agapanthus flower heads, with star-like flowers worked in zigzags fanning out from the centre.

For foreground irises and wisteria, increase and decrease the width of zigzag along the petals. Combine this with parallel rows of straight stitch for iris stems. Notice the colour changes within the wisteria. Try this in shades of yellow for laburnum flowers.

In this picture, the negatives have begun to be put in around the leaf and flower shapes. The technique used to do this depends on the background and the amount of texture needed. This dark stitching will make the light colour in the foxglove stand out and form a strong basis for the foreground embroidery.

Delphiniums

In this project you will embroider a foreground flower in detail, and have a painted background suggesting more of the same flower receding into the distance. The source photograph shows a single flower in detail – use this for reference, and make a pencil sketch to compose the rest of the picture. Trace your design on to tracing paper or acetate ready to transfer on to the silk, or if you are sufficiently confident, draw the design straight on to the silk freehand.

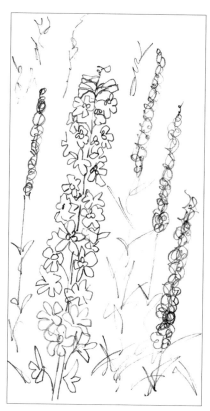

You will need

Resist in a pipette with a nib
Source photograph
Paper and pencil
Ruler
Tracing paper or acetate
Permanent marker for tracing
Air/water-soluble pen
White medium-weight silk
Silk frame, 30 x 25cm (12 x 10in)
Approximately 20 silk pins
Silk paints
Small paintbrush
Mixing palette
Bound 20cm (8in)
   embroidery hoop
Selection of coloured threads
Liquid soap
Iron

To create my composition, I took my source photograph and replaced the background foliage with more delphiniums receding into the background. These I decided to paint on rather than stitch, leaving the foreground delphinium the only embroidered element in the picture.

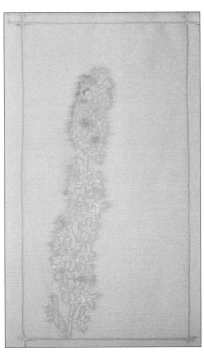

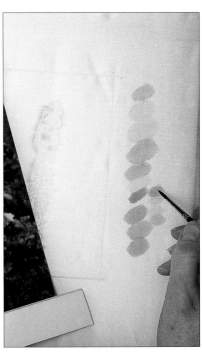

1. Pin your silk to a silk frame and draw in the rectangular frame for your design using a ruler and an air/water-soluble pen. Trace the outline for the design on to the silk by placing your pencil drawing or tracing underneath it. If possible, do this over a light box. Use the photograph for reference.

2. Take away the pencil drawing, then outline the flower shapes in resist. Apply the resist using a pipette. Also outline the rectangular border in order to contain the paint.

3. Using the silk paints, mix a range of blues, purples, greens and pinks. Test the colours on the silk, outside the border. Remember to let them dry. Use your photograph for reference.

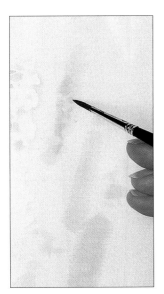

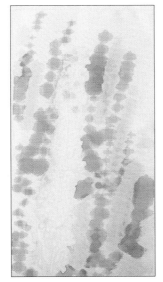

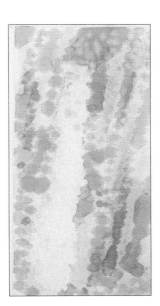

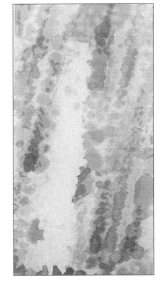

4. Referring to the photograph and your drawing, apply the paint to the silk. Use the brush to dab on the colour and allow it to spread and blend naturally.

5. Gradually build up the colour, starting with the lightest tones and ending with the darkest. If the dyes dry on the fabric they will not blend, so dampen the whole picture with clean water and then paint on to it quickly where you want the colours to merge.

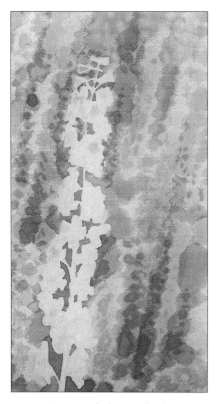

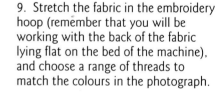

7. Apply dark blue to the inside of each flower. Load a small brush with paint, then hold the brush inside the flower until the paint has spread to fill the shape.

6. Put in some dark areas both around and within the flower to emphasise the edges of the resist.

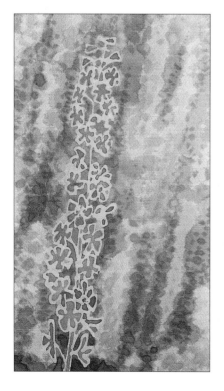

8. Wait for the paint to dry, then iron the fabric for two minutes to fix the dye. Wash the silk in hot, soapy water to remove the resist, rinse in clear water, then iron your work dry to avoid creasing. You are now ready to start your embroidery.

9. Stretch the fabric in the embroidery hoop (remember that you will be working with the back of the fabric lying flat on the bed of the machine), and choose a range of threads to match the colours in the photograph.

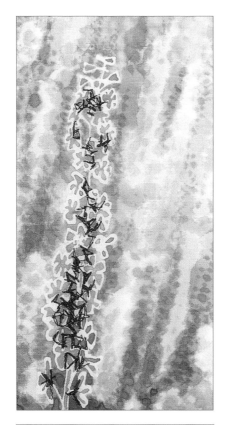
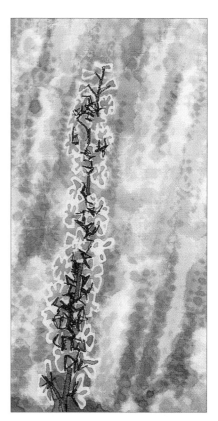

10. Start at the back of the flower head, with the petals that are in shadow. Choose the two darkest shades of purple and use one in the bobbin and the other in the top of the machine. 'Draw in' the negative shapes between the flowers using straight stitch. Trim the connecting threads.

11. For the stems, thread the bobbin with the darker green, and the top of the machine with the lighter green. Tighten the top tension a little so that you can see the bobbin thread more clearly. Using narrow zigzag stitch set to the same width as the stem, work your way down the central stem then along each of the side stems. Trim the connecting threads.

12. For the flowers, thread the top of the machine and the bobbin with the two mid-tone purples. Set the machine on zigzag stitch and increase the tension of the top thread so that the bobbin thread shows on the surface. Make the zigzag stitch as wide as the longest part of the petal, measured from the base of the petal to its tip. (If you are not sure in which direction the needle will go when starting a petal, complete the first stitch by hand.) Fan the stitches outwards from the centre, and rotate the hoop as you go round the flower. Remember to change the width of the zigzag according to the size of the petal you are embroidering, and be careful not to sew over the dark purple stitching you did earlier.

Tip

When your machine is threaded up with two different colours, sew everything you can see in the photograph that requires that colour combination before moving on to the next. This will keep the amount of re-threading to a minimum.

13. Leave the bobbin colour the same, and thread the top of the machine with the lightest tone of purple. Pick out the palest parts of the flower and put in the highlights using zigzag stitch. You may need to sew over some of your previous stitching to link the colours together.

14. Thread the top of the machine with the same mid-tone purple that is in the bobbin, and run through the highlights using straight stitch to blend them in with the other colours. Trim off any connecting threads.

15. To embroider the flower centres, use the darkest purple tone in the bobbin and the off-white in the top of the machine. Set the top tension slightly tighter than normal so that the bobbin colour is visible. Sew three small zigzags in the centre of each flower – one for each of the tiny petals. Snip off the connecting threads.

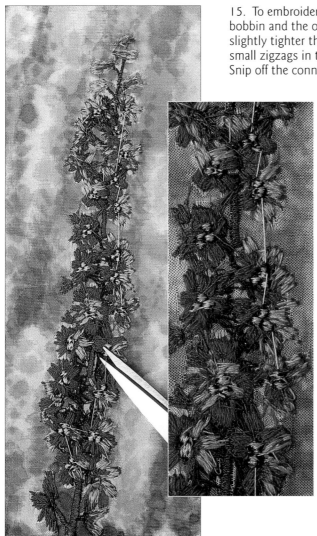

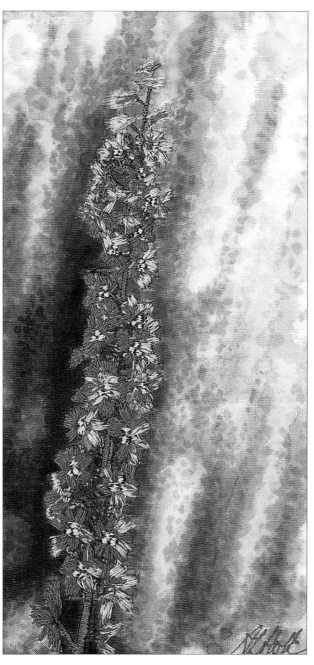

Tip

When reaching the final stages of your embroidery, compare it with your source photograph and sketches to assess whether you have achieved the desired end result. Check the balance of the composition in terms of colour, shape and tone and adjust it if necessary. For example, are the dark areas dark enough? Are the colours strong or light enough?

Delphiniums

When I had completed this embroidery, I decided to strengthen the painted background in order to create more tonal contrast between the background and the embroidered delphinium to make it stand out more.

Verbascum
10 x 18cm (4 x 7in)

The evening light has back lit this verbascum, creating a strong highlight around the petals and buds. This was recreated by pulling an off-white thread in the bobbin to the surface with a tight top tension, and painting the background in strong colours to emphasise the highlight.

Daisies and Grasses
10 x 18cm (4 x 7in)

The softly painted background blends well with the richly embroidered foreground detail.

Datura Lilies
10 x 18cm (4 x 7in)

A painted background of leaves and two other lilies gives depth to this image. This is a good example of 'painting' with stitches in a subtle way, with parallel rows of straight stitch following the shape of the flower.

Blue Irises
10 x 18cm (4 x 7in)

The iris leaves are embroidered using parallel lines of straight stitch, closely observing how the colours change, working from the darkest tones through to the lightest.

Alliums and Tulips

This is a more complex embroidery, needing different skills for each flower and its foliage, and an understanding of how the various elements of the picture fit together to form a coherent design. In this project you will work directly from the source photograph.

You will need

Resist in a pipette with a nib
Source photograph
Paper and pencil
Ruler
Tracing paper
Permanent marker for tracing
Air/water-soluble pen
White medium-weight silk
Silk frame, 30 x 25cm
   (12 x 10in)
Approximately 20 silk pins
Silk paints
Small paintbrushes
Mixing palette
Bound 20cm (8in) embroidery hoop
Selection of coloured threads
Liquid soap
Iron

The source photograph was cropped and only the middle section used for the composition. I then made a sketch showing the various types of foliage and flower shapes, and made notes on which stitches to use for each plant. I decided to use a jagged straight stitch for the background foliage, a spiralling straight stitch with loose bobbin tension for the roses, three parallel blocks of zigzag for the tulip heads and parallel straight stitch for the leaves, blocks of zigzag at various angles for the foreground foliage, spiralling straight stitch in a column for the tall, purple veronica in the foreground, and spiralling straight stitch worked in a spherical shape for the alliums.

1. Begin by pinning the silk to the frame. Place the photograph underneath the silk on a raised surface, so that it is as close to the silk as possible. First draw in a frame for your design using a ruler and the air/water-soluble pen, and then draw in the key elements of the design. Work over a light box if possible. Trace the picture on to tracing paper or acetate if the detail is not visible through the silk.

2. Remove the photograph from underneath the silk and, using the traced elements as a guide, draw in the smaller shapes by eye, using the photograph for reference.

3. Outline the main elements (flower heads and stems) in resist applied using a pipette and nib. Put a line of resist across the picture to mark where the foreground foliage ends and the background begins. Simplify the composition by leaving out any unnecessary detail, such as the tree trunk.

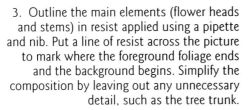

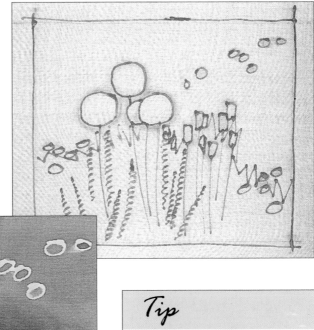

Tip

If you intend to cover the whole of your background with embroidery, you just need a wash of background colour on which to place your stitches.

4. Paint the background using a simple wash of dark and mid green. Let the colour flood up to the lines of resist, but avoid painting over them. Remember this is just the background colour – all the detail will be embroidered.

5. Choose your threads, matching the colours to the photograph. Choose three or four shades for each type of flower, and five or six for the foliage. Select a broad tonal range, from the darkest colour you can identify in the photograph to the lightest. This will make your embroidery more three dimensional; a narrow tonal range results in a 'flat' image.

6. Iron and wash your fabric and stretch it tightly in an embroidery hoop. Thread the top of the machine and the bobbin with the darkest green thread, and set the tension to normal. Identify all the dark green areas (the 'negative shapes') in the photograph and fill them in using straight stitch, echoing the directions and sizes of the leaves. A jagged short stitch will work well for the background, and use long, straight stitches between the iris leaves, for example.

 Tip

To help you identify the darkest areas in a photograph, try turning it upside down – this helps you see shape and tone, without the distraction of content.

7. Leave the dark green in the bobbin and thread the top of the machine with the next lighter shade of green. Make sure you can see the bobbin threads by tightening the top tension. Start putting in the leaf shapes within the dark green area of the background and extending a little way above it. Use straight stitch worked backwards and forwards to create tiny blocks of colour. In the upper part of the picture, work up and down in a random motion to create the impression of foliage in the distance.

Tip

Keep the background foliage simple, creating only the impression of foliage, with no unnecessary detail. This creates a good basis for the foreground flowers.

8. Move the top colour to the bobbin, and thread the top of the machine with the next lighter shade of green. Using the same technique as before, embroider the lighter areas of the picture, overlapping some of the previous stitching and taking it higher up. Trim any connecting threads if you move from one area to another.

Tip

Remember that you are gradually moving from the darkest to the lightest tones, introducing one new thread at a time so a blending effect is achieved.

9. Thread the bobbin with the mid-purple tone, and leave the lighter shade of green in the top of the machine. Create tiny areas of straight stitch sewn in a spiral – the purple in the bobbin will appear as small dots of colour, giving the impression of distant flowers.

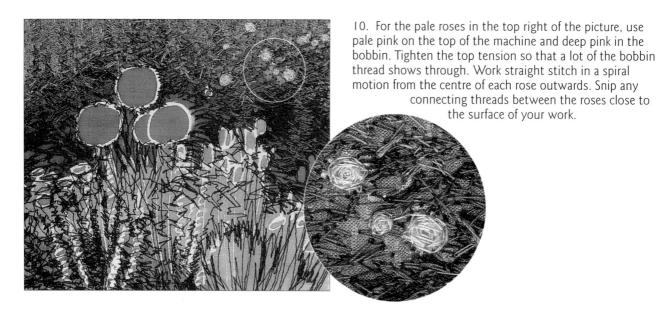

10. For the pale roses in the top right of the picture, use pale pink on the top of the machine and deep pink in the bobbin. Tighten the top tension so that a lot of the bobbin thread shows through. Work straight stitch in a spiral motion from the centre of each rose outwards. Snip any connecting threads between the roses close to the surface of your work.

11. Use the same technique for the darker roses, threading the bobbin with burgundy, and using the mid-tone pink in the top of the machine. For an even darker effect, use dark pink in the bobbin and in the top of the machine. Create a series of roses in various colours and sizes across the picture.

12. For the foreground leaves, use a different set of greens from the background foliage. Use the darkest green in the bobbin, and a mid green in the top of the machine. Make sure the bobbin thread is showing through by tightening the top tension. Using zigzag stitch, work a series of parallel, diagonal stitches across the picture, first in one direction and then in the other to create an impression of leaves.

13. Put in the mid-tone foliage. Put the top colour in the bobbin, and replace the top thread with one a shade lighter. Using the same technique, embroider within and around the previously stitched leaves, taking your stitching higher up the foreground foliage.

14. Put the top colour in the bobbin, and thread the top of the machine with the next shade lighter. Use the same technique to complete the lighter areas of the foreground foliage. Keep referring to the source photograph to identify the detail.

15. Leave the bobbin thread the same and thread the top of the machine with the lightest shade of green. Set the machine on straight stitch, and put in the highlights using sharp, jagged stitches. These will be mainly at the top of the foreground foliage, contrasting well with the dark base of the background and making the foreground stand out.

16. For the dark areas at the base of the allium heads, thread the bobbin with the deepest shade of lilac, and the top of the machine with a shade lighter. Tighten the top tension so that the bobbin thread shows through, and work straight stitch in tight spirals – this technique creates small star shapes that resemble the individual flowers on the allium heads.

17. Leave the same colour in the top of the machine and thread the bobbin with the next shade lighter. Using the same technique, embroider the lighter areas of the alliums. Work your way further up the flowers, partly overlapping the previous stitches.

18. For the lightest areas of the alliums, put off-white in the bobbin and the palest lilac in the top of the machine. Work the highlights at the very top of the flower heads.

19. Replace the off-white in the bobbin with the lightest shade of lilac and blend the highlights with the darker parts of the flower heads by stitching over a small part of each.

20. For the tulip heads, use off-white in the bobbin and cream in the top of the machine. Fill the tulip heads using wide zigzag stitch, giving each flower three petal tips and a rounded base. You will need to work with your design turned sideways.

21. For the sepals, rotate the picture sideways again and sew narrow bands of small zigzag stitches at the base of each flower. Set the tension to normal. Keep off-white in the bobbin, and use the second lightest shade of blue-green in the top of the machine.

22. Next embroider the tall, purple flowers. Use dark purple in the bobbin and a mid purple in the top of the machine. Tighten the top tension so that both threads show, and work a straight stitch up the centre of each flower then spiral back down.

23. Add a highlight down the left-hand side of the purple flower spikes using the same technique. Keep the same colour in the bobbin (this helps the highlight to blend in), and put a paler purple in the top of the machine.

24. Moving now to the tulip leaves in the bottom right-hand corner of the picture, thread the bobbin with the darkest green and the top of the machine with the next shade lighter. Turn your work sideways on and embroider the darkest parts of the leaves using wide zigzag stitch. Move the hoop slowly to keep the stitches closely worked.

25. Repeat this technique higher up the leaves, using the colour from the top of the machine in the bobbin and a shade lighter in the top of the machine.

26. Move the top colour to the bobbin, and replace it with a lighter shade of green. Put in the highlights on the tips of the leaves and the tulip stems. Use fairly long straight stitch so that they stand out against the background.

Alliums and Tulips

I assessed the embroidery at the final stage and added some more roses in the foreground on the right-hand side to balance up the distribution of colour. I used pale pink in the top of the machine and deep pink in the bobbin. I added a few selected highlights to the tulip leaves using the same light green in the top of the machine and the bobbin, and then cut the connecting threads.

Pinks and Lavenders *(Above)*

The leaves in the pot are embroidered by increasing and decreasing the width of zigzag along the length of each leaf. The lavender flowers use a combination of techniques — a spiky straight stitch for the top part of the flower and a compact, spiralled straight stitch for the base. The pinks in the foreground are small zigzag stitches worked from the centre of the flower outwards. The centres are then completed with a small circle of deep pink worked in straight stitch.

A Colourful Corner *(Left)*
21.5 x 26.5cm (8½ x 10½in)

This embroidery is a complex mixture of painted and stitched areas within a highly detailed scene. The spade, water tank and garden shed are painted using the technique of applying a pale wash that is left to dry before darker tones are applied with a small brush. The stitched area includes a wide range of techniques: a varying width of zigzag for the ferns, climbing leaves and white foxglove bells; a jagged straight stitch for the alliums and scabious. This embroidery is based on a garden designed by Nikki Bennett-Jane for the Chelsea Flower Show.

Alliums and Irises
Notice the long stitches used in the foreground grasses. They stand out from the background and add depth to the composition.

Flower Border

This is a project with a wide variety of stitch techniques, although it is simple in its composition. For this picture, you need to be able to identify the negative shapes, for example the dark tones in the foliage. Drawing in the flower heads (the positive shapes) helps with this. It is important to remember to leave spaces in the embroidery for fine details such as the flower heads. If an area is over-stitched, it is difficult to embroider with accuracy.

Turn the hoop sideways to work on the gravel path. You will find that the hoop is easier to move vertically than horizontally, and with better control you will be able to 'draw' the gravel more successfully. In this example, the path has been simplified and embroidered with only a limited number of colours. If you prefer, you can add more detail as gravel comes in many shades and colours.

You will need

Resist in a pipette with a nib
Source photograph
Paper and pencil
Ruler
Tracing paper
Permanent marker for tracing
Air/water-soluble pen
White medium-weight silk
Silk frame, 30 x 25cm (12 x 10in)
Approximately 20 silk pins
Silk paints
Small paintbrushes
Mixing palette
Bound 20cm (8in) embroidery hoop
Selection of coloured threads
Liquid soap
Iron

1. Select the area of the source photograph you want to use for your composition.

2. With an air/water-soluble pen, draw an outline of the composition. Apply resist to all the lines.

3. Wash in green tones for the foliage and the small triangle of lawn in the foreground. Put in a pale beige wash for the steps and path. When dry, add a deeper shade for the shadows across the steps in the distance. Using grey on top and in the bobbin, put in the shadows under the step and at the edge of the gravel path, under the flowers.

4. Using the same grey in the bobbin and a paler grey on top, begin to fill in the gravel path with random straight stitches. Wiggle the hoop a little to avoid straight lines – they should lie in a horizontal direction.

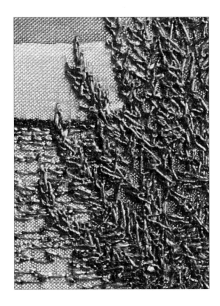

5. Using brown on top and darker brown in the bobbin, put in the woody lavender stems. Change to green and complete the foliage with a straight stitch, zigzagged by hand along the length of the stem.

6. Mark out the position of the large osteospermum flowers. This can be done with permanent marker pen as it will be covered by embroidery. Marking the positions will help you to embroider the negative shapes around the flowers.

7. With very dark green thread on top and in the bobbin, machine in the background around the flower heads. Use straight stitch but direct it diagonally with a slight curve.

8. With straight stitch and using mid-green in the bobbin and sage green on top, machine in the foliage of the aubrietia behind the osteospermums. Use small stitches to create distance.

9. With a narrow zigzag stitch and using deep pink on top and in the bobbin, machine in the heads of the flowers.

10. Change to mid pink in the bobbin and pale pink on top and complete the details of the aubrieta flowers.

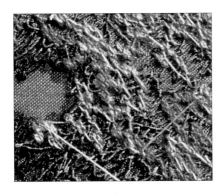

11. When moving between areas of stitching which are the same colour, carry the thread over the work and snip the trailing thread later to separate the groups of flowers – see page 00 for details of the method.

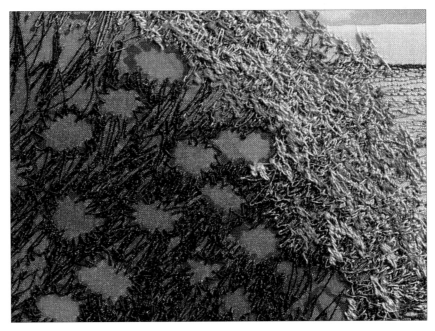

12. With a straight stitch, run between the foliage using a slightly lighter green on top and a very light green in the bobbin to put in the highlights, and to separate the flowerheads a little.

13. With straight stitch and using two different shades of green, put in foliage between the gaps left for the osteospermums.

14. With white on top and in the bobbin for some flowers and white in the bobbin and lilac on top for others, put in the petals using a wide zigzag stitch. As each petal is completed, rotate the hoop slightly and work the next, so they fan out from the centre.

15. With deep pink in the bobbin and yellow on top, and with a small zigzag stitch worked on the spot, put in the centres of the osteospermum flowers. Use a small zigzag stitch for the petals of the small white snow-in-summer (*Ceratium tomentosum*) flowers. Change to pale pink and add the final details of the aubrietia where it breaks through between the other flowers.

16. With green on top and in the bobbin, use rows of straight stitches to embroider the triangle of lawn.

17. With very pale blue-green on top and in the bobbin, put in a few random straight stitches at the base of the border, which will add highlights to the foliage and have the effect of separating the small white flowers. Check the balance of the composition and adjust if necessary.

Flower Border
Actual size
The finished embroidery.

The Artist's Garden
Actual size

*My garden is an endless source of inspiration. I used artistic licence to replace
a plant that had finished flowering with osteospermums. The scale of stitching
is important: small straight stitches and tiny zigzag stitches were used for
the delphiniums, roses and the Alchemilla mollis in the background. The
stronger, bolder zigzag treatment and the increase in scale of the penstemon and
osteospermum in the foreground adds depth.*

The Rose Arch

Actual size

The path is a mixture of painted shadows and straight stitch to emphasise the paving stones. This leads your eye into the picture through a wide range of greenery and foliage to the sunlight beyond the gate. Zigzag stitch has been used in the foreground to give larger-scale leaves and flowers. The distant foliage is a tiny straight stitch.

Trees & woodlands

I love my regular walks through local woodlands; there is so much to be inspired by, and the changing seasons feed my passion for interpreting nature in machine embroidery all year round. As winter snowdrops fade away, they are soon replaced by primroses and daffodils. There is freshness and vitality to this time of year, with bright green ferns unfurling and fresh new buds everywhere. For me, yellow is the colour of spring; even the new shoots on the trees are a lime or yellow-green. I eagerly look for other signs of spring such as blossom, bluebells and wild garlic, adding more colours to the landscape. As the seasons progress, azaleas and rhododendrons, which my garden has in abundance, change the palette to reds, purples, pinks and orange.

The summer brings trees in full leaf, creating dappled shadows on the dry, dusty pathways of last autumn's fallen leaves. Strong tones, dark shadows and bright sunlight provide dramatic contrasts, and the richly coloured, mossy trees, woodland streams, ferns and dense foliage provide a vast range of greens that are a great source of inspiration to me.

When autumn arrives the leaves start to change colour; green turns to yellow then rust, red and orange. This is a very exciting time in terms of colour, texture and detail. Swathes of bracken slowly change to subtle shades of brown, contrasting with the grassy paths and silver birch trees. There is a feeling of richness and warmth in the colour palette that belies the onset of winter.

As winter leaf-fall reveals the bare branches of the trees, you become aware of the patterns formed by the branches, and the angles and shapes between them. When highlighted by frost and snow, coupled with a blue sky and winter sunlight, an inspiring scene is created. When snow falls I brave the cold as quickly as

Snow Shadows
10 x 23cm (4 x 9in)

The strong blue shadows across the snow create perspective and depth in this winter woodland scene.

possible to try to get the perfect photograph. I look for foreground interest, texture, contrast, strong silhouettes and features that draw my eye into the distance, creating depth and perspective. There is a limited palette at this time of year, but copper beech and oak trees, bracken and fallen leaves provide some colour, as do strong, blue shadows stretching across fallen snow – my favourite subject for a winter scene!

The Mossy Stream
18 x 25.5cm (7 x 10in)

The texture of the moss is captured here by using tiny, closely worked stitches.

Tree trunks

Tree trunks are usually the strongest feature of a woodland scene. To recreate the huge variety of textures, colours and shapes, there are numerous different machine embroidery techniques that you can use – which you choose depends on how much detail you can observe, and the colour and texture of the bark. To give them a rounded appearance, use the darkest tones down the side of the trunk that is in shadow, and gradually introduce lighter tones as you move round to the side that is facing the sun.

Perspective

To help achieve a sense of perspective, use smaller stitches, a less textured finish and more muted colours as trees diminish in size into the distance. The techniques on these two pages are suitable for various tree types.

This textured foreground tree bark has been created using a series of vertical rows of zigzag stitch, in which the stitch width has been increased and decreased several times along the length of the trunk. A dark bobbin thread, pulled to the surface by increasing the top tension, has been used throughout, and the colour of the top thread has been varied to obtain the gradual change from light to dark.

Autumn in Candy Woods
7.5 x 13cm (3 x 5in)

The main tree trunk was created using vertical, parallel lines of straight stitch, and the background trees were worked in narrow columns of zigzag stitch.

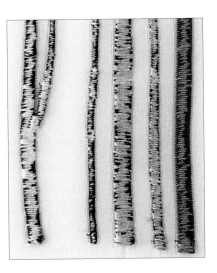

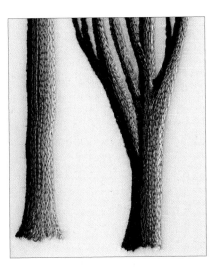

These distant trunks are worked as vertical columns of zigzag stitch, sometimes with a line of straight stitch underneath. The bobbin thread is pulled to the surface by a tight top tension and a darker thread is used in the bobbin than on the top of the machine.

Middle-distance trunks are worked as vertical columns of medium-width zigzag stitch with the bobbin thread pulled to the surface by a tight top tension. Notice the different effects that can be achieved by using different thread colour combinations.

These smooth foreground tree trunks consist of parallel rows of straight stitch worked vertically, in progressively lighter shades as you move across from left to right.

Foreground moss-covered tree trunk

1. Begin by working the dark side of the trunk using a dark brown thread in the bobbin and on the top of the machine. Use parallel lines of straight stitching and follow the curve of the trunk. Make small, jagged, up and down movements of the hoop as you work to create wavy lines of stitching.

2. Work the mossy areas using a dark green thread on the top of the machine and yellow in the bobbin. Use straight stitch and move the hoop as before, tightening the top tension to pull the bobbin thread up and create a three-dimensional, textured effect.

3. For the lightest areas, place a lighter yellow in the bobbin and continue working the same stitch to complete the trunk. Remember to curve the lines of stitching around the trunk.

To create a smooth-textured, mossy bark, place the moss-coloured thread in the bobbin and pull it up with a tight top thread. Use parallel lines of straight stitching and vary the shade of the top thread to create areas of light and dark.

This silver textured bark uses a similar technique to that shown on page 92, but with straight stitching worked between the sections of zigzag stitching to add more texture and fill in the gaps.

Foreground lichen-covered tree trunk

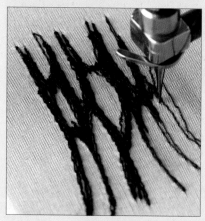

1. First sew the bare bark. Use rows of straight stitching and follow the pattern of the bark, using your source photograph for reference.

2. Replace the bobbin thread with a blue-green, tighten the top tension and loosen the bobbin tension to create loops of bobbin thread on the surface. Work short, jagged straight stitches in between the brown.

3. Continue to fill the spaces in between the bare areas of bark. Use a lighter coloured thread on the top and in the bobbin on one side of the tree to create shading.

Woodland floor

Fallen leaves are often a feature of woodlands and the techniques used to create them vary with distance from the foreground; the scale of the stitches creates a sense of perspective.

Distant woodland floor.

Distance

For a woodland floor viewed in the distance, work parallel lines of straight stitch in various colour combinations to form stripes, representing shadows from the trees and foliage.

Middle distance

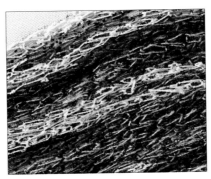

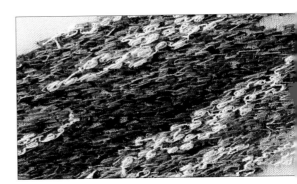

1. Work the middle-distance woodland floor as rows of spiralling straight stitch. Begin by working the base with a dark thread on the top and in the bobbin.

2. Gradually introduce different shades and colours until the area is completely filled. Create shaded areas using the darker tones.

This middle-distance area of woodland floor is created by setting the machine on a narrow zigzag stitch and working series of stitches worked on the spot to create individual leaves. Place the rows of stitching in curved, parallel lines, following the contours of the ground.

Foreground

1. Beginning with the darkest colour, work each fallen leaf as a series of zigzag stitches worked on the spot. Leave spaces in between for leaves of other colours.

2. Fill in the gaps using different colours, working through the mid tones to the highlights. Work the stitches in different directions by changing the angle of the hoop.

Foliage

Within densely stitched foliage, the depth of the scene can be expressed by the scale of the stitching. Here are some examples of this.

Distant foliage

Middle-distance and background foliage is worked in curved lines, mimicking the shape of the branches. In each example below, the top tension is tightened to pull up the bobbin thread, and there is a darker shade in the bobbin than on the top.

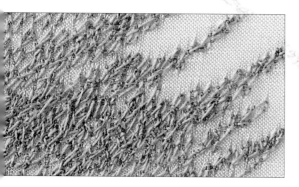

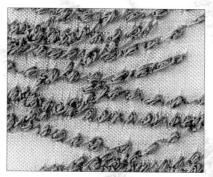

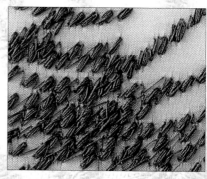

A less textured finish suggests background foliage. Here, straight stitching has been worked in curved lines with small, spiralling movements of the hoop.

For less distant foliage, use curved lines of small zigzag stitches, with some stitches worked on top of each other to suggest individual leaves.

This middle-distance foliage is worked in the same way as that shown on the left, but with a larger stitch.

Foreground foliage

1. Work straight stitch along the stem to the tip of the leaf, then work back again using zigzag stitch, gradually increasing the width of the stitch to form the top part of the leaf.

2. Complete the leaf by gradually reducing the width of the zigzag stitch, then work the next leaf in the same way.

Different-shaped individual leaves can be created using this method. For larger leaves, work two sections side by side, rotating the hoop so they sit at an angle to each other. Use with the same colour on the top and in the bobbin, or place a darker shade in the bobbin, to create different effects.

Ferns

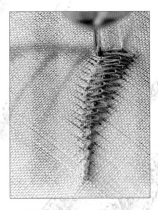 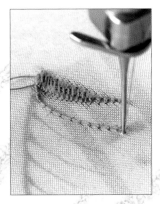

1. Working from the base of the fern to the tip, stitch along the midrib of the first frond using straight stitch, then work back along it using a widening zigzag.

2. When you reach the stem, change back to straight stitch and work the next frond in the same way. Note: rotate the hoop so that the straight stitching lies vertically under the machine and work the zigzag stitch horizontally across it.

3. Work to the tip of the fern to complete. Observe the shapes of the ferns, and how the fronds gradually diminish in size towards the top and end with a delicate curl at the tip.

Grass

Various techniques can be used for grasses, depending on whether they are in the fore-, middle- or background.

These distant grasses were created using straight stitch worked up and down in vertical and diagonal lines. For more depth, place a few curved blades of grass in front, worked on top of the background grass in a darker shade of green.

For foreground grass, work from the base of each blade of grass with straight stitch, then work back down it with a zigzag, gradually increasing the width of the stitch as you approach the base.

Rosebay willow herb

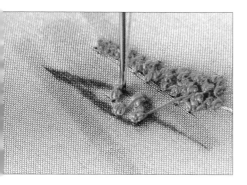

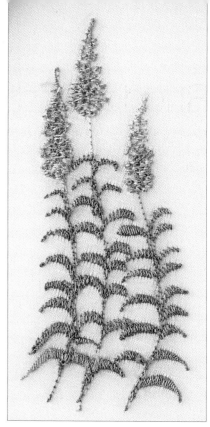

Starting at the base of the flower, create a series of zigzags worked on the spot. Gradually reduce the stitch width as you approach the top of the flower, then increase it again as you work your way back down, filling in the gaps as you go. A darker shade in the bobbin makes the flower look more three-dimensional.

The leaves of the rosebay willow herb are worked in the same way as the foreground foliage on page 96.

Foxgloves and bluebells

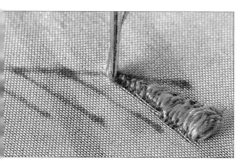

1. To create foxgloves, first draw in the stem and a guide line for each trumpet. Use a darker shade in the bobbin than on the top of the machine and tighten the top tension. Work straight stitches from the stem to the end of the first trumpet. Change to a wide zigzag stitch and work back towards the stem, reducing the stitch width as you go to form the trumpet shape.

2. Change back to a straight stitch, sew along the stem and work the next trumpet in the same way.

Completed foxglove flowers; for the stems and leaves, see the rosebay willow herb above.

Bluebells (shown right) are worked in a similar way to foxgloves, but with a constant width of zigzag. This time, however, draw only a single curved line for each flower, then stitch the individual bells by eye. Using a narrow zigzag stitch, work from the top of the stem to the tip of the first bell and back again to the stem, then continue down the stem making a total of five or six bells on each flower.

Rhododendrons

Begin by drawing in the outline of each flower. With a darker shade in the bobbin and a tight top tension to pull the bobbin thread to the surface, work each flower as a series of zigzag stitches radiating out from the base. Reduce the size of the background flowers to create perspective.

Vary the colour and size of the flowers to give depth and added interest to your embroidery. Notice how the angle of the flowers is also important for achieving a realistic effect.

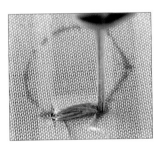

1. Starting at the base on the left of the flower, use a wide zigzag stitch and sew on the spot to create the first petal.

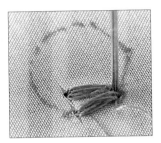

2. With the needle at the base of the flower, work the next petal in the same way, rotating the hoop a little so that the petals begin to fan out from the base.

3. Complete the first row of petals.

4. Work the remaining rows in the same way, dovetailing each row with the preceding one.

Daffodils

Growing in groups or drifts in a woodland setting, creating daffodils is more about swathes of colour rather than individual flowers (see page 7).

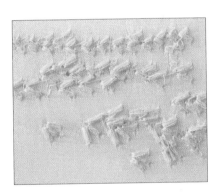

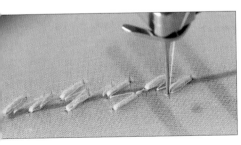

1. For a cluster of flowers, sew all the petals that lie at the same angle first. Use a wide zigzag stitch and sew on the spot for each petal.

2. Rotate the hoop slightly to alter the angle of the stitching, and add a second petal to each flowerhead.

Completed daffodil heads. If trumpets are required, work these as narrower zigzag stitches laid horizontally and worked in a different shade of yellow.

Sunlit Path

The strong tonal contrast drew my eye to this scene; the bright sunlight creates wonderful dark shadows, and flashes of dramatic light cutting through the trees form stripes across the woodland path. The dark brown tree trunks form strong verticals, and contrast with the lush greens and yellows of the summer foliage.

Working from the background to the foreground section by section, allow areas to overlap a little to create the illusion of depth. Remember that depth can also be achieved by altering the scale of the stitching (smaller stitches in the distance and larger, more textured stitching at the front of the picture).

You will need

Resist in a pipette with a fine nib

Full-size copy of the source photograph (or a similar one of your own)

Ruler

Paper, pencil, permanent marker tracing paper and/or acetate for tracing (optional)

Air/water-soluble pen

White, medium-weight silk

Wooden silk frame, 30 x 25cm (12 x 10in)

Approximately 20 silk pins

Paintbrushes, silk paints and mixing palette

Liquid soap

Iron

Bound 20cm (8in) embroidery hoop

Selection of coloured machine embroidery threads

Source photograph
Cropping this photograph emphasises the tall tree on the left-hand side. The final size is 10 x 18cm (4 x 7in).

1. Pin the silk on the silk frame, then draw in the border and the main elements in the photograph using an air/water-soluble pen – the foreground tree and its main branches, the ground level, the main areas of foliage and the round patch of light at the bottom on the right of the picture. Compare your drawing with the photograph and, once you are happy with the composition, go over the purple lines with resist and allow it to dry.

Tip

Here I have transferred the design by drawing it freehand directly on to the silk, referring closely to the photograph, but the method you use is entirely up to you (see page 37). If you are not happy with your drawing, add any extra details you feel are needed, or leave out some of the detail to simplify the picture.

2. Mix a very pale yellow to match the lightest background colour you can see. Apply the colour to the background, behind the trees and over the round light patch, to give the whole picture a warm glow. Create a yellow-green mix and 'dot in' the mid-green areas of foliage.

3. Mix a darker yellow-green and put in the darker areas within the foliage. This will help you observe where the different areas of colour are in the picture.

4. Use a strong mix of black and brown for the tree trunks and branches, and a dilute version of the same mix for the ground. When the paint has dried completely, fix it in the normal way (see page 39).

6. Starting with the round patch of sunlight bottom right, place white in the bobbin and a pale yellow-green on the top. Work the darkest areas in the centre and on either side using diagonal rows of tiny straight stitches. For the lighter areas, pull the bobbin thread up by tightening the tension on the top of the machine. Add highlights by placing white on the top of the machine and sewing in between the existing stitching.

5. Place your work in a bound 20cm (8in) hoop and select your thread colours, using the photograph and the painted background as reference.

Tip

You will need a wide range of yellow-greens for the more distant areas, a smaller range of blue-greens for the foreground foliage, and a selection of dark and warm browns for the tree trunks and woodland floor.

7. Using white in the bobbin and pale yellow on the top of the machine, put in the back lighting. Stitching in between the foliage, use straight stitches worked with small spiralling movements in diagonal and horizontal curves.

102

8. For the mid-tone areas of background foliage, put a bright yellow-green on the machine and a paler version in the bobbin. Fill the mid-tone areas using straight stitch and tiny spiralling movements of the hoop, working back and forth across the embroidery. Avoid stitching over the tree trunks.

9. Put a very dark brown thread on the top and in the bobbin, and stitch parallel rows of straight stitch up and down the background tree trunks. Use the same colours for the shadows behind the trees and the dark shadow lying across the path below the round patch of sunlight.

10. For the dark foliage in the distance, either side of the path, put a very dark green on the top of the machine and in the bobbin. For a delicate look, work numerous tiny straight stitches, as in step 8, leaving sufficient space within the stitched areas for the background to show through. Allow these stitches to overlap the round patch of sunlight.

11. Use the same yellow-greens as those used in step 8 – the paler version on the top and the brighter one in the bobbin. Continue placing the mid tones within the lower areas of background foliage, this time stitching across the tree trunks to bring the foliage forward, and using small spiralling stitches to create texture. Stitch the strip of bright green grass along the distant edge of the bank in the same way.

Tip

Woodland scenes may require the lighter tones to be stitched first, depending on the layering of the elements from front to back. In this case the sunlit areas of foliage in the background need to be worked before the darker foreground areas.

12. Continuing within the same area, including the grassy bank, place the pale yellow-green in the bobbin and pale yellow on the top of the machine, and put in the lighter tones.

13. Leave the same colour in the bobbin and place the bright yellow-green on the top, and work the darker areas higher up on the background foliage.

Tip

Follow the line and shape of the branches when stitching the foliage, referring constantly to the photograph, to produce a realistic effect. Draw in as many guide lines as you need with the air/water-soluble pen.

14. With dark brown in the bobbin and a mid-tone brown on the top, begin to stitch the woodland floor – the lighter area lying just beyond the shaft of light, and the mid-tone areas in the foreground. Towards the front of the picture, use larger stitches worked in spiralling movements to create more texture and depth.

15. Place white thread in the bobbin and on the top of the machine and work the brightest sunlit areas of the woodland floor. Use horizontal rows of straight stitch where the main shaft of light crosses the path, jagged straight stitches on the bank, and tiny, spiralling stitches for the smaller patch of light towards the foreground.

105

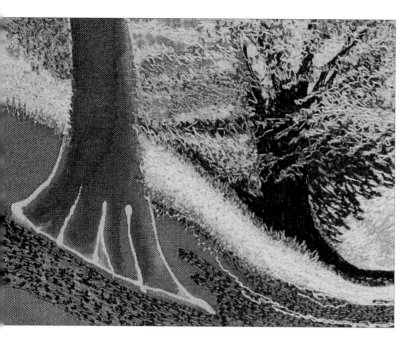

16. Replace the top thread with a bright yellow-green and put in the strip of grass along the edge of the sunlit area toward the front of the picture. Use small, jagged stitches to mimic the blades of grass.

17. Now work the darkest areas of the woodland floor, and the main tree trunk and branches. Place a very dark brown on the top of the machine and in the bobbin (see step 9). Use lines of straight stitch for the shadows on the bank, changing to spiralling stitches as you approach the path to blend with the lighter areas of ground. Sew the tree trunk and branches in sections using parallel lines of straight stitch (flat colour is required here, because the tree is in shadow). Avoid the lighter parts of the roots.

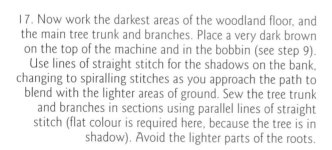

18. Replace the top colour with a mid brown, and place the lighter highlights down the right-hand side of the trunk and the vertical branches, and on the roots. Use the same colours to blend together the lighter and darker parts of the ground you have already stitched.

19. Change to a very dark green on the top and yellow in the bobbin, and stitch the dark areas of foreground foliage. The inclusion of yellow helps break up the lines of stitching, and this, coupled with the use of tiny stitches and small, spiralling movements of the hoop, produces a delicate, lacy effect.

20. Move the very dark green to the bobbin and place a mid green on the top. Using the same technique, stitch the lighter areas of foreground foliage, blending them with the darker tones that went in first.

21. Using yellow in the bobbin and lime green on the top of the machine, strengthen the sunlit parts of the foliage. Use the same technique as in steps 19 and 20 to fill small, sunlit patches within the foliage.

Tip

As you get to the end of your embroidery, assess and compare the balance and quantity of colours with the source photograph. To aid this process, place both the embroidery and the photograph upside down and view them from a short distance.

The completed embroidery.

Spring Walk
13 x 18cm (5 x 7in)

This picture works, even though I have broken a design rule and placed the trees in the centre of the composition. The horizontal and diagonal lines are also an important aspect of the design of this embroidery.

Mossy Tree
13 x 18cm (5 x 7in)

*A smooth trunk on the foreground tree was worked with parallel lines of straight stitch. The lichen
was added last using a light grey bobbin thread pulled to the surface to provide a little texture.*

Fallen Leaves

A strong tree dominates this scene, with its foliage trailing down to the ground on the right. The path, sweeping away to the left, leads the eye into the distance past an avenue of beech trees. Rich autumnal colours and textures made this composition irresistible.

To transfer the design and paint the background, follow the steps on pages 37 to 39.

You will need

Resist in a pipette with a fine nib

Full-size copy of the source photograph (or a similar one of your own)

Ruler

Paper, pencil, permanent marker tracing paper and/or acetate for tracing (optional)

Air/water-soluble pen

White, medium-weight silk

Wooden silk frame, 30 x 25cm (12 x 10in)

Approximately 20 silk pins

Paintbrushes, silk paints and mixing palette

Liquid soap

Iron

Bound 20cm (8in) embroidery hoop

Selection of coloured machine embroidery threads

Source photograph

I took sections from two photographs of the same scene to compose this embroidery, placing the tree in the centre of the picture and retaining the pathway on the left. The composite photograph shown here is reproduced at two-thirds of its actual size.

Tip

You nearly always stitch the darkest tones first and work towards the lightest, so it is a good idea to load a number of bobbins with the darkest tone of each colour before you begin.

Make sure you select a broad tonal range of each colour.

1. Once you have washed and ironed your work to fix the image (see page 39), stretch it in a 20cm (8in) embroidery hoop so that the left-hand side of the design falls within the hoop, as this is the side you will embroider first. Select a good range of threads, matching them to the photograph and to the painted background.

2. Start with the darkest areas first, starting with those beneath the yellow background foliage. Place a very dark green in the bobbin and dark green on the top, and fill the area with tiny, spiralling straight stitches. Take the stitching up into the lower parts of the foliage using a more open stitch.

3. Move to the darkest areas of the woodland floor. Place dark brown in the bobbin and a soft mid brown on the top, and sew horizontal, parallel rows of small straight stitches, following the curve of the ground. Work from the background forwards, changing to a longer stitch as you approach the foreground worked in a tight spiralling movement to create texture. Also work the shadows beneath the three trees in the background.

4. Put the soft mid brown in the bobbin and a light, golden brown on the top of the machine, and use the same stitch to fill in the lighter areas of ground.

5. Complete the ground by working your way through three or four further colour combinations, finishing with the highlights. Each time, move the top colour to the bobbin and place a lighter shade on the top.

6. For the background tree trunks, work parallel rows of straight stitches using dark brown in the bobbin and on the top. Replace the top colour with a green-brown and place a line of stitching down the centre of each trunk. Finally, change to a paler brown on the top and stitch the highlight down the right-hand side.

7. Place a deep, golden yellow on the top of the machine and a mid blue-green in the bobbin, and work the darker shades within the yellow background foliage. Work lines of straight stitching, some spiralled, on a curve from left to right.

8. Place three or four more layers of stitching, working progressively lighter areas by moving the top colour to the bobbin and placing a lighter shade on the top. Finish with a very pale yellow on the top for the highlights. Carefully overlap the tree trunks and the dark green stitching behind them.

Tip

If the palest tone you have selected does not stand out as strongly as you would like, replace the bobbin thread with white.

9. Moving to the large shrub, place very dark green on the top and in the bobbin, and work the darkest areas at the base and in the middle using spiralling straight stitches.

10. Keep the very dark green in the bobbin and place a bright mid green on the top, and work the mid-tone areas in the same way. For the lightest parts of the shrub, mainly at the top, move the top colour to the bobbin and replace it with a light green.

11. Having completed the right-hand side of the embroidery, move the hoop to the right and complete the pale green foliage on the right of the picture using the same threads. For the distant foliage behind the branches of the main tree, use light green on the top and white in the bobbin, and work tiny, spiralling straight stitches to give the impression of distance. Do not work the stitches too densely – allow the sky to show through.

12. Complete the small area of ground on the right (see steps 3 to 5). For the main tree, place a very dark brown on the top and in the bobbin. Sew several parallel rows of stitching down the left-hand side of the trunk, working top to bottom. Replace the top colour with dark brown and fill the middle portion of the trunk using the same stitch. Also stitch in the main branches, using straight stitch for the finer branches and zigzag stitch for the broader ones. Adjust the width of the zigzag depending on the width of the branch, and place the finest branches first.

13. Move the dark brown to the bobbin and place a lighter brown on the top, and stitch the mid-tone areas towards the right-hand side of the tree trunk. For the lightest areas, place the top colour in the bobbin and a lighter shade still on the top. Use the same threads to sew the wispiest branches, using straight stitch. Change the top colour to mid green and work the lichen-covered, lower part of the tree trunk. Work in rows, following the curve of the roots. The brown thread in the bobbin helps blend the colour with the rest of the trunk.

14. Place the foreground leaves on the main tree, starting with the darkest ones. For these, use dark yellow on the top and in the bobbin, and set the machine to zigzag stitch. Hold the hoop still while you work each leaf, allowing the zigzag stitch to build up into the form of a leaf. Work different-sized leaves, and vary the direction in which they lie. Refer to the photograph as you work.

15. Put a strong mid yellow on the top, retaining the same colour in the bobbin, and stitch the lighter leaves in the same way. Finally, move the strong mid yellow to the bobbin and place a paler yellow on the top for the palest leaves, most of which are at the top of the tree. Use the widest zigzag setting to make the large foreground leaves.

The completed embroidery.

Autumn Walk
16.5 x 25.5cm (6½ x 10in)

Rich autumnal reds, yellows and greens give this scene huge visual impact.

An Autumn Journey
10 x 18cm (4 x 7in)

The colour of the tree trunks and foliage becomes paler in the distance.

The Richness of Autumn
18 x 13cm (7 x 5in)

With only a few leaves left to fall, all the autumn shades are on the woodland floor in this embroidery.

Winter Snow

The blue sky and shadows, dark grey trees and snow-covered hawthorn trees make this a striking winter composition. A limited palette, and therefore the smallest number of threads, was selected for this project, and there is the opportunity to practise your freehand painting skills (see pages 40–42).

You will need

Resist in a pipette with a fine nib

Full-size copy of the source photograph (or a similar one of your own)

Ruler

Paper, pencil, permanent marker tracing paper and/or acetate for tracing (optional)

Air/water-soluble pen

White, medium-weight silk

Wooden silk frame, 30 x 25cm (12 x 10in)

Approximately 20 silk pins

Paintbrushes, silk paints and mixing palette

Liquid soap

Iron

Bound 20cm (8in) embroidery hoop

Selection of coloured machine embroidery threads

Source photograph
There is an even proportion of painted and stitched areas in this picture, both of equal importance. This photograph is reproduced full-size.

1. Pin the silk on the silk frame, and draw in the main elements using an air/water-soluble pen. Begin by breaking the composition down into three areas of colour, then adding just the bases of the shrubs in the foreground. Go over the lines with resist and allow it to dry completely.

2. Paint the sky by laying progressively darker bands of colour from the horizon upwards, starting with clear water, and allowing the colours to blend naturally on the silk. Place lines of resist where bands of sunlight are shining through the trees in the distance. This will leave white lines on the silk once the resist is removed.

3. Paint the central blue area, making the mix more dilute as you approach the foreground, and the light green area at the front of the picture.

4. Change to a very small brush, and add patches of blue-grey to the area lying behind the trees on the distant slope. Build up the colour gradually using tiny dots of paint rather than sweeping movements of the brush. Finally, draw in the background tree trunks, and the two trees and the fence in the mid-ground (these will not be stitched and will therefore remain part of the background).

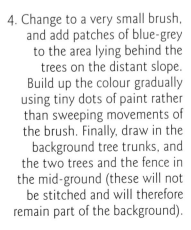

5. Once you have ironed and then washed your painting to fix the image, stretch it in a 20cm (8in) hoop and select your threads, referring to both the photograph and the painted background.

6. Stitch the most distant trees with a very pale blue in the bobbin and very dark grey on the top (the pale bobbin thread will help break up the lines of stitching and produce a delicate, lacy effect). Draw in the branches first using tiny straight stitches, starting at the top and working downwards into the trunks.

7. Replace the bobbin thread with dark blue and, using straight stitch, work the hedge running along the horizon from the right, and the trees growing further down the hillside.

8. Place mid blue in the bobbin (retaining the very dark grey on the top) and soften the trunks into the background by placing horizontal rows of straight stitch between them to represent the shadows. Add more small trees to the left and within the main woodland area. Finally, use straight stitch for the boundary at the base of the slope.

9. Replace the bobbin thread with pale blue, and use tiny, spiralling straight stitches for the darker areas of foliage on the two trees in the middle distance. Stitch the snow-covered branches in the same way, using pale blue on the top and white in the bobbin.

10. Moving further down the picture, draw in the dark trees on the right using spiralling straight stitches. Use the very dark grey in the bobbin and dark olive green on the top.

11. Change to mid olive green in the bobbin and soft white on the top, and stitch the snow-covered ground lying behind the foreground trees. Use rows of straight stitch, running parallel with the slope of the ground. Allow the green-painted silk to show through the stitching, like the grass underneath the snow. Leave gaps for the foreground shrubs.

12. Returning to the very dark grey, place this colour both on top and in the bobbin and stitch the stems and branches of the foreground shrubs. Draw them first using straight stitch, then strengthen the thicker branches and trunks with zigzag stitch.

13. Place mid olive green in the bobbin and dark olive green on top, and stitch the lighter-coloured branches of the hawthorns. Use the same method as before.

14. For the snow on the branches, use pale olive green on the top of the machine and soft white in the bobbin. Loosen the bobbin tension so that plenty of the white thread shows through, resembling snow. Set the machine on straight stitch, and work along the boughs in horizontal curves using small, spiralling stitches.

15. Replace the top thread with bright white, and put in the bright snow on the top of the hawthorns using the same spiralling stitching worked in small, curved shapes.

16. Using the same threads, work diagonal lines of zigzag stitching across the ground at the front of the picture, following the angle of the slope. Leave gaps in the stitching so that the green background shows through, and overlap the bases of the shrubs to firmly embed them in the ground.

17. With a mid olive green in the bobbin and a light olive green on the top, use small straight stitches worked in vertical jagged lines to fill in the grass patches in the foreground.

The completed embroidery.

Sitting on the Fence
18 x 13cm (7 x 5in)

Soft, painted detail for the distant fields gives great depth to this composition. Strong tonal contrast in the foreground, within the tree, fence and shadows on the snow, adds to this sense of perspective.

Springtime

The focal point of this embroidery is the beautiful splash of colour created by the woodland azalea. The embroidery is worked from the back of the picture to the front. Carefully complete each area before moving forwards to the next, overlapping the stitches as you proceed to push the details back and create depth. In the foreground the stitches will be bolder and larger, standing out against the more delicately worked background areas.

I have transferred the design by drawing it freehand directly on to the silk, referring closely to the photograph, but the method you use is entirely up to you (see page 37).

You will need

Resist in a pipette with a fine nib

Full-size copy of the source photograph (or a similar one of your own)

Ruler

Paper, pencil, permanent marker tracing paper and/or acetate for tracing (optional)

Air/water-soluble pen

White, medium-weight silk

Wooden silk frame, 30 x 25cm (12 x 10in)

Approximately 20 silk pins

Paintbrushes, silk paints and mixing palette

Liquid soap

Iron

Bound 20cm (8in) embroidery hoop

Selection of coloured machine embroidery threads

Source photograph

This embroidery is based on the photograph shown on the left without cropping or alteration, as I was happy with the composition. It offers the opportunity for many different techniques, including small, spiralling straight stitches for distant foliage; smooth, closely worked zigzags for tree trunks; large, jagged stitches for the foreground leaves and flowers; and delicately stitched detail for the fern at the base of the tree. This photograph is reproduced at two-thirds of its actual size.

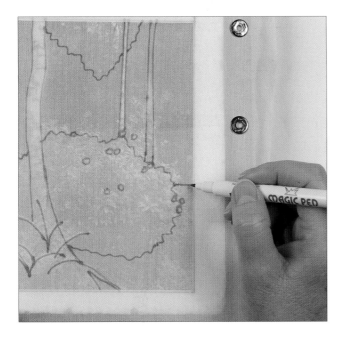

1. Begin by pinning the silk on the wooden frame, then draw in the border and the main elements in the photograph using an air/water-soluble pen. Begin with the three main tree trunks, then outline the azalea bush and mark in the positions of the main flowers (more flowers can be added when you start to sew). Put in a guide line down the centre of each fern at the base of the foreground tree, and draw in the tree line, slightly lower than in the photograph, to open up the sky a little more. Finally, indicate the positions of the background trees as single lines, and add any details on the ground you can see. Once you are happy with the composition, go over the purple lines with resist and allow it to dry.

Tip

This embroidery is too large to fit in the embroidery hoop, so stretch up the top half first as this is where you need to start.

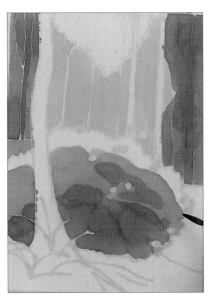

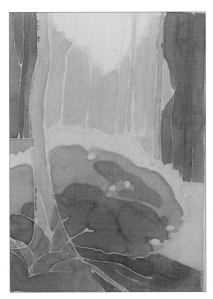

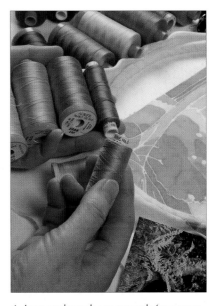

2. Paint the background, beginning with a flat wash of pale yellow-green for the lighter areas of foliage in the background. (Not all of this area will be stitched, so choose the lightest shade visible.) Mix a darker green for the darker areas of foliage and for the lower half of the azalea bush, and a mid green for the upper half. Be careful not to paint over the spaces left for the flowers.

3. Add some more yellow to the pale yellow-green mix for the green areas of ground, and for the spaces left for the flowers, and use a watery mix of black and purple for the tree trunks. Finally, make a mustard-coloured mix for the moss at the base of the tree and the ferns, and add some brown for the area of bare ground beneath the azalea. Allow the paint to dry thoroughly.

4. Iron and wash your work (see page 37), and stretch it in a 20cm (8in) bound embroidery hoop so that the top part of the picture lies within the hoop ready for stitching. Using the background and the photograph for reference, choose a good range of coloured threads (see page 17).

5. Using the darkest green both on the machine and in the bobbin, work the darkest areas of the background. Set the machine on straight stitch, and move the hoop using small, spiralling movements to create texture. Leave gaps for the mid to lighter tones.

6. Leaving the bobbin colour the same, thread a mid-tone green on the machine and use the same stitch to place the mid tones. Overlap the darker areas of stitching slightly to blend them together, and use the lower edge of the stitched foliage to outline the foreground shrub as accurately as possible.

7. Using a very dark brown in the bobbin and a light brown on the top, work the background tree trunks using a narrow zigzag stitch. Start at the base of each trunk and work upwards, tapering the top slightly by making the stitch narrower. Use the same stitch to put in the main branches, working from the trunk towards the end of each branch, tapering down to a straight stitch in some cases.

Tip

Always cut off the connecting threads before changing to a different colour.

8. Place the mid-tone green in the bobbin and a lighter, silvery green on the machine, and stitch the lighter areas of foliage as before (steps 5 and 6).

Tip

Remember to refer continually to the source photograph to ensure that the colours and composition remain true to the original. Draw in extra guide lines using the air/water-soluble pen if necessary.

9. Stitch foliage around some of the branches and across the sky, overlapping some of the background tree trunks. Keep these stitches tiny so that they recede into the distance. Retain accurate outlines around the foreground elements (in this case the main tree trunk on the left and the shrub) to maintain their size and shape.

10. For the main tree trunks on the right, use grey thread in the bobbin and white on the machine. Work them from the bottom upwards using a wide zigzag stitch. Change to a white bobbin thread, and use a narrower zigzag to place a white highlight down the right-hand side of each tree. Take it only halfway up the tree in the mid-ground.

11. Using mid green in the bobbin and light green on the machine, stitch the foliage overlaying the top of the right-hand tree. Make the stitches larger than before so that they stand out from the background.

12. Add highlights to this foliage and to the shrubs on the right using the light, silvery green in the bobbin and an even paler green on the top. Use straight stitch and move the hoop using jagged movements to create a series of 'V' shapes, so that it looks different from the distant foliage.

13. Work the top part of the main foreground trunk as three overlapping columns of zigzag stitch, using the same threads as before (step 10). This time, tighten the top tension so that more of the bobbin colour shows through.

14. Place a white highlight down the right-hand side (see step 10).

15. Put the grey back in the bobbin and put a darker grey on the top, and use straight stitch to place the dark markings going across the trunk with small, horizontal stitches.

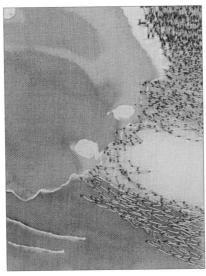

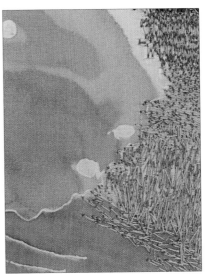

16. Move the fabric in the hoop so that the lower part of the embroidery lies within it. Stitch the small area of grass on the right, just below the trees, using the mid green in the bobbin and the light, silvery green used in step 12 on the top. Use straight stitch and work in horizontal rows, moving the hoop up and down sharply to create small, jagged stitches.

17. Work the areas of bare ground to the right of the azalea using a light, pinky brown on the top and a darker tone in the bobbin. Work in straight stitch back and forth across the work, following the slope of the ground.

18. For the grassy patch near the foreground, use a more yellowy green. Put a dark tone in the bobbin and a mid tone on the top of the machine, and repeat the jagged straight stitches you used in step 16, making them slightly longer. Put the mid tone in the bobbin and a lighter tone on the top, and add a few highlights using the same stitch.

19. Using the air/water-soluble pen, draw in the outlines of the main light-coloured leaves on the azalea for guidance.

Tip

Your original design is for guidance only; adapt it, if necessary, as your work progresses, and draw in extra detail if required.

20. Stitch the darkest areas between the leaves you have drawn on, avoiding the spaces left for the flowers and the lines drawn for the ferns. Use dark green in the bobbin and in the top of the machine and sew around the leaf shapes using small, jagged straight stitches.

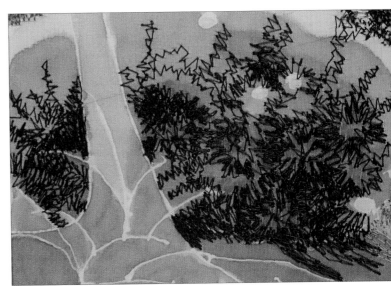

21. Leave dark green in the bobbin and place mid green on the top. Work the shapes at the top of the shrub using the same stitch as before, and the mid-tone leaves lower down. For each leaf, use three or four straight stitches worked back and forth on the same spot. To make larger stitches, run the machine slowly and move your hands more quickly.

22. Move the mid green to the bobbin and place a paler green on top, and work the lighter leaves higher up on the azalea. Complete the shrub by stitching the lightest-coloured leaves at the top using the paler green in the bobbin and a pale silvery green on the top. Remember to leave spaces for the flowers.

23. For the darkest flowers, use the darkest shade of pink in the bobbin and a mid-tone pink on top of the machine. Work each flower using spiky straight stitches. Add more flowers, if you wish, for more colour. Move the mid tone to the bobbin and place a lighter tone on the top for the light pink flowers towards the top of the bush.

24. Complete the main tree trunk using the same method as before (see steps 13 to 15). Take the highlight approximately two-thirds of the way down. Finish by placing a few bands of straight stitching across the trunk using pale lilac thread in the top of the machine and grey in the bobbin.

25. For the area underneath the azalea, place a very dark brown in the bobbin and a dark brown on the top. Work small, spiralling straight stitches in curved rows, following the roots of the tree and the slope of the ground. Use the same colours for the dark areas behind the ferns. Work these in jagged lines of straight stitching to define the fronds.

26. With two shades of pinky brown as before (see step 17), work the lighter areas using the same technique. Overlap the darker areas slightly so that they blend together.

27. Change to a pale mustard yellow on the top of the machine and a deeper version in the bobbin, and work the moss covering the lower part of the main trunk. Use straight stitches worked in compact, wavy lines.

28. For the ferns, place dark green in the bobbin and a fresh blue-green on the top. Lay a foundation of dark leaves for the lighter leaves to stand out against, worked using jagged lines of straight stitching (as in step 25).

29. Move the blue-green to the bobbin and place a light yellowy green on top, and place the mid-tone ferns. Work each frond by straight stitching from the base to the end of the frond, then zigzagging back again. Increase the width of the stitch towards the stem.

30. Complete the ferns by replacing the bobbin thread with off-white and stitching the foreground leaves. Use the same stitches as before, and refer closely to the photograph to ensure the correct positioning and angle of the leaves.

The completed embroidery.

Rhododendrons at Highfield
18 x 13cm (7 x 5in)

Always a riot of colour in the springtime, this corner of my garden has been an inspiration for many of my embroideries.

Lake Vyrnwy Woodland
18 x 13cm (7 x 5in)

The bright yellow-green foliage, typical of spring, and glimpses of a distant azalea, make this embroidery a favourite for this time of year.

Daffodils
18 x 10cm (7 x 4in)

Viewed through the carefully stitched gate, the background trees and walls are painted on the silk. The quantity of stitch increases towards the foreground, culminating in the heavily embroidered daffodils and their foliage.

Over the Fence
18 x 13cm (7 x 5in)

The fence posts and trees diminish in size towards the back of the picture, creating depth.

Spring Woodland
Actual size

Unusually, the trees in the distance are zigzagged, which on this larger scale works well. The moss gives the foreground trees so much texture, and to recreate this I have used a straight stitch with a tight top tension, which has pulled the yellow bobbin thread to the surface to create the highlight.

Index

The Lower Falls

18 x 13cm (7 x 5in)

The foreground water is painted, contrasting well with the texture of the moss-covered rocks, foliage and waterfall.

Delphiniums and Roses
8 x 8cm (3 x 3in)

A wide range of techniques was used for this small, detailed embroidery.